WORLD WAR II
INFANTRY

IN COLOUR PHOTOGRAPHS

LAURENT MIROUZE

The Crowood Press

POLISH INFANTRYMAN, SEPTEMBER 1939 CAMPAIGN

A t the end of World War I Poland regained her independence as a sovereign state. Her first army was made up of many contingents originally raised, equipped and armed by the different belligerent nations of 1914-18.

At the beginning of the 1930s the army's first efforts at uniformity were overtaken by a radical new issue of uniforms, equipment and weapons, selected after wide-ranging trials. The new khaki uniforms were notably modern in design; and the personal equipment was partly derived from the current equivalents in service with the German army.

Despite the forward-looking design of much of their equipment, however, the 39 Polish infantry divisions were unable to resist for long the German steamroller which smashed through Poland's borders in September 1939. After three heroic weeks their resistance – partly sabotaged by Russia's treacherous agreement to partition Poland with Germany – was beaten down. However, more than a quarter of a million Polish fighting men would escape to continue the struggle alongside the Allies on other fronts.

1—M1931 helmet, in nickel-chrome-molybdenum steel, painted in a khaki shade, with powdered cork added to the paint while wet to produce a matt finish; the shade was known as 'salamander'. The leather interior harness of this, one of the most modern helmet designs of the period, was derived from that of the old German M1916, with small adjustable pads to alter the fit.

2—The M1936 tunic was of a single cut for all ranks, and of a khaki shade described as 'grey-brown-green'. The seven front buttons bore the 1927 crowned eagle national emblem. Rank insignia and unit ciphers were worn on the shoulder straps; the collar bore patches in branch-of-service colours, with the traditional Polish zig-zag edging. On campaign only the insignia of rank were retained.

3—M1936 belt, in tan leather with a single-prong buckle, the same for all branches.

4—Two triple cartridge pouches in tan leather, modelled on the German World I design. Each pocket held three five-round clips of 7.9mm ammunition, giving a total of 90 rounds.

5—Entrenching tool in tan leather carrier, to which was attached the leather M1931 bayonet frog, which accommodated different types of bayonet then in Polish army use; the one illustrated is the M1929.

6—Haversack M1933 in proofed khaki canvas; it could be carried either slung around the body to the right side, or attached to the left side of the belt. Normal contents were the soldier's washing kit and small personal effects, emergency rations, and a hand grenade.

7—M1932 knapsack, of heavy canvas, its shoulder straps linked to the cartridge pouches at the front. External stowage comprised the rolled greatcoat and blanket, and sometimes a tent section, strapped round the sides, and the aluminium mess tin of German pattern strapped to the flap. The tent section was sometimes carried inside the pack, with a change of underclothes, shirt and socks, laces, rifle cleaning kit, etc.

8—M1932 gasmask in its khaki canvas satchel; some troops still carried the French ARS mask, which the Polish type was in the process of replacing at the outbreak of war.

9—M1937 trousers, of the same khaki shade as the tunic, confined at the ankle by short puttees.

10—M1934 boots in natural tan leather; regulations of 1935 had prescribed that these should normally be blacked, but many were still in their natural finish at the time of the mobilisation of 1939. Unlike most contemporary military boots they had the soles screwed on, rather than sewn, and thus gave superior protection against damp.

11—M1929 Mauser rifle, a Polish variant of the classic German 98k. Of 7.9mm calibre, it was manufactured in government factories at Warsaw and Radom. Many captured rifles were salvaged for use by the Wehrmacht after the Polish defeat.

GERMAN INFANTRYMAN, FRENCH CAMPAIGN, MAY-JUNE 1940

The appearance of the German soldier in the French campaign represented a late stage in the evolution of the field grey uniform which first appeared in 1907. Since the organisation of the *Reichsheer* in 1919 the uniform had been identical for all German states; and the colour remained field grey. A new design appeared in 1935, together with a new helmet, but the cut did not differ greatly from previous models. The personal equipment, too, while brought up to date, showed a clear line of development from the items issued during the Great War. In accordance with Hilter's wishes the smartness of the uniform was enhanced by the adoption of a richly varied system of emblems, badges and other distinctions.

In May-June 1940 the *'Landser'* of the German *Wehrmacht* was a formidable infantryman, well armed and equipped, and provided with the means of transport which made possible the fast-moving *'Blitzkrieg'* warfare which gained Germany her first great victories.

1—M1935 helmet; of 1.2mm thick steel, it was painted matt slate grey. The M1931 lining comprised leather segments mounted on an adjustable ring. Originally the standard army helmet bore two insignia decals: a tricolour shield in slanted stripes of the national colours (black, white, red), and a silver-grey eagle on a black shield. From May 1940 the new slate grey paint finish was supposed to be applied over the tricolour shield for better concealment, and only the eagle decal is illustrated here (although the tricolour shield did survive in many cases).

2—M1933 cotton collar, attached to the inside of the tunic collar by five buttons. It was reversible, white on one side and green on the other, the former being exposed with walking-out uniform and the latter with campaign dress. By regulation, a centimetre's depth was supposed to show above the tunic.

3—Removable shoulder straps, the examples illustrated being of the type made in the period 1938-40. Of dark green cloth with a piping in the branch-of-service colour (white for the infantry), they bore the regimental cipher in the pre-war period. After the outbreak of war the ciphers were either covered by a cloth loop, or omitted during manufacture, for obvious reasons of security.

4—M1935 field grey tunic, fastening with five buttons, and provided with four pleated pockets fastened by buttoned flaps. The collar, of dark blueish green, bore two 'lace' patches, their design being a simplified form of traditional Prussian collar lace. The design was common to all branches, except for two narrow lengths of branch-colour lace. Before the introduction of the M1939 leather equipment suspenders the tunic had interior fabric suspenders linked to small hooks protruding through eyelets in the cloth to help support the weight of the belt. Above the right breast pocket was sewn the national emblem of an eagle clutching a wreathed swastika. Rank chevrons identifying junior NCOs – here, those of a senior corporal – were sewn to the left sleeve only.

5—Oilcloth satchel, attached to the gasmask sling or canister, containing a chemically-treated anti-gas cape.

6—M1933 cartridge pouches, in two sets of three, each set containing six five-round clips of 7.92mm Mauser cartridges. The pouches were of black leather with a 'pebbled' finish.

7—Gasmask canister M1930, in fluted metal painted grey-green. It contains a fabric gasmask with a screw-on metal filter.

8—Black leather bayonet frog, with M1884-98 Mauser bayonet.

9—Entrenching tool in artificial leather carrier, whose strap both holds the head of the tool and confines the bayonet scabbard to stop it flapping.

10—M1931 tent section/shelter half. This *'Zeltbahn'*, of proofed cotton cloth with a three-colour camouflage pattern on both sides, is roughly triangular; it has a central slit, and can be worn as a poncho, or buttoned to others to make a campaign tent.

11—M1931 'breadbag' haversack in olive fabric; normal contents included washing kit, weapon cleaning kit, emergency rations, eating utensils, field cap, etc.

12—M1931 mess tin, of aluminium painted grey-green.

13—The M1931 water bottle, with a capacity of roughly 1½ pints, is covered with felt fabric, and has a black-painted aluminium cup fixed over the neck.

14—'Stone-grey' trousers; these had two slash side pockets closed by buttons, one right rear pocket and one small fob pocket in the right front.

15—Black leather marching boots.

16—Mauser 98k rifle, 7.92mm calibre.

17—M1924 hand grenade.

7

FRENCH INFANTRYMAN, FRENCH CAMPAIGN, MAY-JUNE 1940

When the French army was mobilised in September 1939, the men of the infantry could have walked out of a 1918 photograph, with the sole major difference of wearing khaki rather than horizon blue. The image of the victor of the Great War, familiar from a thousand bronze war memorials, seemed stamped into the military mentality.

The equipment of the infantryman, which had been criticised since the turn of the century, had certainly been the subject of a number of detail reforms: M1935 equipment with a knapsack of soft canvas rather than rigidly framed material; MAS36 rifle; M1938 uniform. But although these innovations had been partially introduced by the spring of 1940, the French foot-slogger still faced the light, mobile German infantry weighed down by a heavy greatcoat recalling the Franco-Prussian War, and an overweight and over-complex harness.

1—The manganese-steel M1926 helmet followed the general form of the 1915 Adrian helmet. The applied insignia on the front varied according to the branch of service; for the infantry it was a flaming grenade.

2—M1935 khaki shirt and tie. The soldier might also wear a light pullover (M1936) under the greatcoat, but not the tunic – this had been withdrawn from the campaign uniform in 1937 in an effort to lighten the soldier's load.

3—Greatcoat M1920/35, double-breasted, with two rows of six khaki-painted buttons. The new M1938 greatcoat, single-breasted with five large front buttons, had been issued to some troops by this date. The collar patches bear the regimental cipher enclosed by two dark blue pipings; note also the citation lanyard in yellow and green, awarded to the 69th Fortress Infantry Regiment, and a 1939 *Croix de Guerre* awarded to this soldier. A single rolled shoulder strap, designed to prevent equipment straps slipping, is worn on the right: officially each man should have had two.

4—M1935 personal equipment. Made up of linked items, it represented a real step forward from the old equipment with its rigid wood-framed knapsack, and its plethora of equipment slings crossing on the chest. Unfortunately, only about one third of the French infantry had received the new system by spring 1940. It incorporated a standard issue belt, M1903/14, and shoulder suspenders, M1892/14.

5—Two M1935/37 cartridge pouches were worn at the front of the belt, carrying a total of 90 rounds. The third pouch of the old equipment, carried on the rear centre of the belt, was replaced by a triangular leather loop which engaged with the rear central strap of the suspender system.

6—The water bottle M1935 held about 3½ pints.

7—M1935 haversack, normally containing mess tins and mug, eating utensils, daily rations, and spare ammunition for the section light machine gun.

8—Upper knapsack M1935, containing reserve rations, washing and mending kit, pullover, blanket, field cap, etc.; the side pockets could accommodate light machine gun magazines. A lower knapsack M1935 – not illustrated here – could be attached below this upper pack, and carried spare clothing.

9—The tent section M1935, square in shape, had a central slit allowing it to be worn as a poncho.

10—Entrenching tool, here the M1916 shovel, in the M1935 leather carrier.

11—ANP31 gasmask in its carrying satchel; like the British model, it had a tube connecting the mask to a filter which remained in the satchel when the mask was put on.

12—M1938 trousers, the so-called 'pantalon golf'. They reflected contemporary fashion, but were less than satisfactory in the field, and tore easily. In 1940 about half the infantry still had the M1920/35 'pantalon culotte', fastened at the knee.

13—Puttees; although laced gaiters were put into production in 1940, few reached the troops before the Armistice.

14—Hobnailed M1917 ankle boots.

15—1907/15 M16 'Berthier' rifle, in 8mm Lebel calibre. Nicknamed 'fishing rod' because of its length, this old weapon still equipped the majority of the infantry in 1940, alongside the M16 carbine derived from it. The long cruciform bayonet was carried on the left side of the belt, and is hidden here by the turnback of the greatcoat.

François Vauvillier

9

SCOTTISH INFANTRYMAN, FRANCE, FEBRUARY 1940

This soldier of the Argyll and Sutherland Highlanders, who disembarked in France in January 1940 during the freezing but relatively inactive winter of the 'Phoney War', differs little in general appearance from his predecessors of 1918. Despite the introduction of new items of uniform and equipment from 1937 onwards, the traditional 'tribal items' of the Highland soldier are still represented. After the arrival of the British Expeditionary Force in France, orders were issued banning the future issue of the kilt to troops going overseas; but photographs show that the 'Jocks' clung to their traditional garment for a while, despite its unsuitability for modern warfare.

The 51st Highland Division suffered terrible losses in the course of the bitter fighting retreat to the Channel. The 7th Argylls were almost wiped out, and the survivors finally went into captivity after a heroic last stand near St. Valéry-en-Caux.

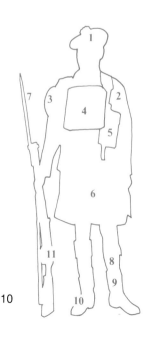

1—Balmoral bonnet in khaki serge, with the regimental badge pinned through a patch of tartan on the left side.

2—Battledress blouse. The original model, as here, had all buttons concealed by flies except for those on the shoulder strap. Regulations forbidding the display of insignia in the field were at this time generally obeyed, although not universally. The use of an improvised scarf may appear unconvincing, but at least one photograph of Highlanders taken at this time confirms it; the khaki flannel shirt was collarless, and the neck of the rough serge blouse chafed the skin.

3—Steel helmet Mk.II, painted semi-matt green or brown. The sprung fabric and webbing chinstrap and the interior harness were obviously different from those of the Great War Mk.I; the shape was less obviously modified, the brim being flatter and the skull circular rather than ovoid.

4—'Small box respirator' or gasmask, here in the 'alert' position, slung on the chest by a neck strap and held steady by a cord round the chest. The rubber and fabric mask was attached by a corrugated rubber tube to the box filter, which remained in its pocket inside the satchel when the mask was put on.

5—M1937 personal equipment in cotton webbing. The different items were all linked, in an attempt to spread their weight. Supported by both the belt and the shoulder suspenders are a pair of 'basic pouches': each could accommodate either a folded cotton bandolier of 50 rounds for the .303in. rifle and a couple of hand grenades, or two magazines for the section's Bren light machine gun, or two bombs for the platoon's 2in. mortar. The entrenching tool head was carried in a webbing pouch, to which the tool's haft was buckled, attached below the belt at the rear. The felt-covered enamelled water bottle also buckled to the ends of the shoulder suspenders, carried down through buckles on the belt. A haversack or 'small pack' could be attached either behind the shoulders, or to the ends of the shoulder suspenders on the left hip.

6—Kilt – for the Argylls, in '42nd (Government)' sett – and drab cloth campaign cover. By the battles of late spring most if not all Highlanders in Maj.Gen. Fortune's 51st Division had substituted the trousers of the Battledress uniform. Sporrans were not worn.

7—Bayonet No.1 Mk.I; this new nomenclature was applied to the basically identical sword bayonet carried since before the Great War.

8—'Hose tops' – footless stockings worn in addition to the issue ankle socks by kilted units, the turned-down tops traditionally decorated with garter-flashes in regimental colours.

9—'Anklets web', of webbing with internal leather reinforcement and fastened by two buckled straps, which replaced the old puttees with the introduction of the 1937 uniform and equipment.

10—'Ammunition boots', sturdily made in pebble-finish blackened leather, and heavily hob-nailed.

11—Rifle No.1 Mk.III*, the Short Magazine Lee Enfield of .303in. calibre used by the British infantryman since the Great War. This bolt-action weapon, with a removable magazine holding ten rounds, was robust, reliable, expensively made, and in the hands of a trained man was capable of accurate and surprisingly rapid fire.

Philippe Charbonnier

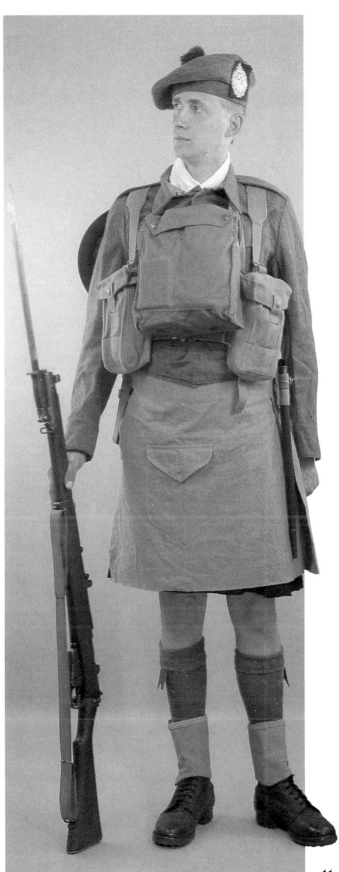

BELGIAN INFANTRYMAN, MAY-JUNE 1940

In 1915 the Belgian army adapted itself, for better or worse, to trench warfare, discarding its old coloured uniforms for a less conspicuous khaki outfit supplied from British sources. With the adoption of the Adrian helmet the Belgian soldier, who also wore a greatcoat with turned-back skirts, acquired a very French appearance, which had changed little by 1940. The new uniform adopted in 1935 displayed only slight modifications of the Great War version.

The personal equipment, introduced shortly after the Great War, followed the general outlines of the German equivalent: triple ammunition pouches, an individual haversack, slung water bottle, etc. At the time of Belgian mobilisation some troops were issued with the M1915 Mills equipment. Like his French comrade, the Belgian infantryman faced the fast-moving *Wehrmacht* in an outfit too heavy and cumbrous for modern warfare.

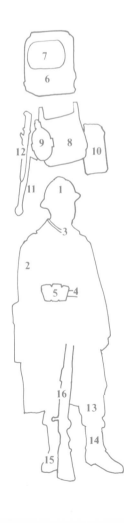

1—M1931 helmet in manganese-steel, painted khaki – an almost exact copy of the French M1926, apart from the more horizontal angle of the brim at front and back, and the black leather internal harness. The front bore the lion-head emblem of the Belgian army for all branches of service.

2—Khaki M1935 greatcoat, with two rows of five large buttons bearing the lion device. It had two side pockets with straight buttoned flaps, and two vertical rear pockets below the half-belt. The skirts had a central rear vent; in marching order, as illustrated, the fronts were buttoned back to free the legs. The grenade insignia on the collar identify a regiment of Grenadiers, and the shoulder straps bear the regimental cipher below a small grenade. The tunic was worn under the greatcoat in the Belgian army.

3—Cotton collar, giving some protection against the chafing of the heavy coat cloth.

4—Tan leather belt with adjustable buckle; personal variations were not uncommon.

5—Tan leather ammunition pouches, copied from German models, each of the three pockets holding three five-round clips, giving a total capacity of 90 rounds.

6—M1930 knapsack, made of a heavy light khaki fabric on a bamboo frame, with leather shoulder straps and webbing stowage straps. Four loops on the flap allowed the attachment of the mess tin as illustrated; straps on the sides secured the rolled blanket and spare boots.

7—Mess tin of khaki-painted aluminium, with loops allowing it to be strapped to the equipment.

8—Haversack, copied from the German 'bread-bag', with external fittings for one or two water bottles; of heavy cloth, it could be carried slung around the body on a strap. It contained rations and some spare clothing.

9—Aluminium water bottle covered in khaki cloth, with a cork stopper. A leather strap sewn to the cover allowed it to be attached to the haversack.

10—New model gasmask, carried in a slung satchel. Like the British model, the rubber face mask was attached by a tube to the filter carried permanently in the satchel.

11—Entrenching tool in tan leather belt-carrier; there were several models, often with a strap holding the bayonet scabbard to the tool in the German fashion.

12—Tan leather bayonet frog; and M1916/35 bayonet, its hilt secured by a strap.

13—M1935 khaki trousers, straight-cut, with two slanting side pockets and a right rear pocket. The trousers were supported by braces.

14—Black leather gaiters, laced up the front by means of seven metal hooks.

15—Blackened leather boots.

16—M35 Mauser rifle of 7.65mm calibre – as in many smaller armies of the period, a nationally manufactured version of the German issue rifle.

13

ITALIAN ALPINE INFANTRYMAN, FRANCE, JUNE 1940

In 1940 six of the Italian army's 73 divisions were classed as 'Alpine'. The formation of these special troops was a natural response to Italy's rugged terrain, and particularly to the fact that her northern frontier passes through some of the greatest mountain massifs in Europe.

The uniform of these *'Alpini'* differed little from that of the ordinary infantry except in their special headgear and insignia; they also received specialised equipment in the form of nailed boots, a Tyrolian-style pack, the alpenstock, climbing ropes and crampons, etc. Considered as crack troops, the *Alpini* were sent against France's *Chasseurs Alpins* during Mussolini's pointless campaign of 10-25 June 1940 – a stab in the back of a country already locked in desperate battle against the German invaders, and a campaign which produced meagre results due to inadequate leadership and logistics.

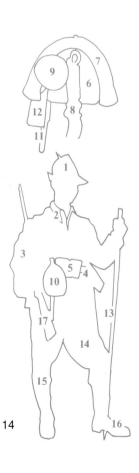

1—The felt Alpine hat, introduced into the army in 1910 and still in use today. As the jaunty trademark of the *Alpini*, it was only with reluctance laid aside for a steel helmet in combat. The black crow's feather was fixed by a pompon in battalion colour; white for the 1st Bn. in each regiment, red for the 2nd, green for the 3rd and blue for the 4th. The badge on the front, embroidered in black thread on grey-green cloth, consisted of a flying eagle over a bugle-horn and crossed rifles. In the curl of the bugle-horn the regimental number was displayed – here, the 3rd.

2—M1939 shirt, in grey-green flannel or lighter material according to the season, and universal issue throughout the army. It had two breast pockets, and a two-button front vent down to mid-chest level. It was often worn with a tie, normally grey-green but of different colours in some units.

3—M1940 tunic, in the grey-green adopted for Italian army uniforms in 1909. This four-pocket, open-collar design was common to most branches of service; note the integral cloth belt with two buttons. Junior NCOs' sleeve rank insignia were embroidered in red on a grey-green ground – here, the chevrons of a corporal. Branch-of-service collar patches were in distinctive colours, and shaped as two- or three-point 'flames' – here, the green of mountain troops, with the white metal star of Savoy which appeared on all Italian army collar patches.

4—M1891 belt of grey-green leather, its single-prong buckle worn at one side to permit the wearing of the ammunition pouches centrally at the front.

5—M1907 double cartridge pouch in grey-green leather, each pocket holding four clips of 6.5mm ammunition for the Carcano rifle. The weight was partly supported by the M1891 suspender, which passed round the neck.

6—M1939 mountain troops' pack, in heavy fabric. This capacious pack has two large exterior pockets, and five fabric straps allow the stowage of a greatcoat, a blanket, and/or a tent section in camouflage material. This very popular pack was also issued to some ordinary infantry formations.

7—Grey-green single-breasted greatcoat, rolled and stowed around the pack in regulation fashion.

8—Climbing rope.

9—M1933 steel helmet, painted grey-green, bearing the stencilled badge of the Alpini and the regimental number. This helmet was sometimes seen with a fitting on the side allowing the attachment of the Alpine troops' traditional pompon and feather plume.

10—Water bottle, in aluminium covered with grey-green cloth; it was issued in one-litre (1¾ pint) and two-litre (3½ pint) sizes, the larger type being illustrated here.

11—Bayonet frog and M1891 entrenching tool carrier, here containing a combination pick/shovel.

12—Model T35 gasmask, carried in a cylindrical cloth bag, the size being marked in Roman numerals on the outside of the bag.

13—Ash-wood M1934 alpenstock.

14—M1940 grey-green trousers, in the full, straight, ankle-length cut issued to Alpine troops.

15—Standard puttees.

16—M1912 mountain boots, with special nails for climbing.

17—M1891 Carcano rifle in 6.5mm calibre.

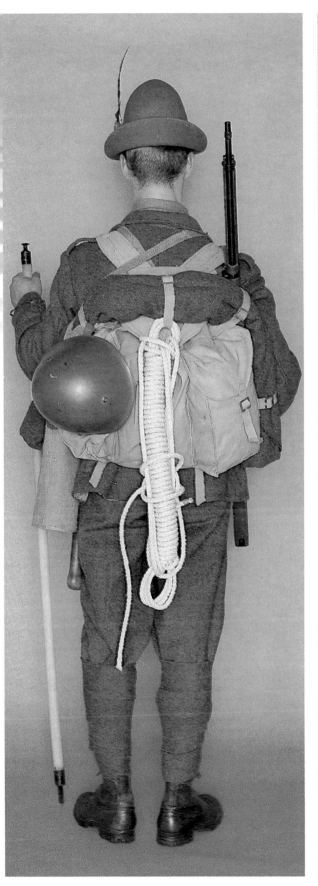

GERMAN INFANTRYMAN, LIBYAN CAMPAIGN, FEBRUARY 1941

Responding to the appeals of his Italian allies, repeatedly and expensively defeated by far smaller British forces in North Africa, Hitler assembled and despatched a *Wehrmacht* expeditionary corps, which disembarked at Tripoli in February 1941. The German army's experience of tropical campaigning was limited to minor colonial operations long before, and they faced the task of preparing 'from scratch' for a new and challenging theatre of operations.

Responsibility for designing a new uniform was given to the Hamburg Tropical Institute. Under pressure of time, the Institute supposedly chose to take the British army in India as its model; but if so, the wrong lessons were drawn. The uniform worn by the *Afrika Korps* in their first battles consisted of a sun helmet; a cotton tunic, cut rather too snugly for comfort; and half-breeches resembling jodhpurs. This outfit was quickly modified in the light of desert experience, and more loose-fitting and practical alternatives were found.

1—M1940 tropical helmet in cork covered with olive cloth. A painted metal shield was pinned to each side, echoing the decals of the steel helmet: on the right, the national colours in slanting stripes, and on the left the eagle and swastika emblem of the Heer (army).

2—Tropical shirt in olive cotton, with a four-button front and two large breast pockets.

3—Tie in olive cotton – hardly ever seen in the front line.

4—Removable shoulder straps, made in the same cloth as the uniform, with the usual '*Waffenfarbe*' — branch-of-service colour piping round the edge. Rose pink identified armoured units, including some motorised anti-tank troops within the Panzer divisions.

5—M1940 tropical tunic in olive cotton; the four pockets resembled those of the woollen European uniform. The collar 'lace' followed the design of that on the European uniform, but in dull blue and brown, with no variation between branches of service. The national eagle above the right breast was also in blue on brown. The left breast bears the bronze 'assault badge' awarded to participants in at least three actions; at this stage the motorised troops and armour crews of the Panzer divisions shared the same design.

6—Shoulder suspenders for infantry equipment, in olive cotton webbing apart from a reinforcement of leather at the point of junction high on the back. Various hooks and rings allowed the braces to be attached to the ammunition pouches and belt, and the attachment of the assault equipment to the harness behind the shoulders.

7—Standard issue ammunition pouches.

8—Olive webbing version of the standard bayonet frog.

9—M1884/98 Mauser bayonet.

10—Olive webbing belt, with a standard buckle plate painted olive.

11—Entrenching tool, here in standard issue black leather carrier.

12—Webbing frame, whose stowage straps allowed the attachment of various combinations of assault equipment. Here the M1931 mess tin is carried above the rolled M1931 camouflaged *Zeltbahn*, and a cloth bag containing a sweater, rations, tent pegs, and rifle cleaning kit.

13—M1931 'breadbag'. Apart from the normal contents, it would here contain the olive cotton tropical field service cap, inspired by the type then worn by the German mountain troops.

14—Tropical water bottle, made of aluminium covered with a compound of vulcanised fibre and wood, which gave better insulation from the climate; for the same reason the cup fitted over the neck was made of bakelite.

15—M1940 olive cotton tropical trousers, laced at the calf; they have two slanted slash side pockets and a front fob pocket.

16—High laced leather and canvas tropical boots; this old-fashioned design was soon generally abandoned in favour of ankle boots of the same materials.

17—Mauser 98k rifle, 7.92mm calibre.

BRITISH INFANTRYMAN, NORTH AFRICA, SPRING 1942

This NCO of the 50th (Northumbrian) Division represents an 8th Army soldier at the time of Rommel's May/June offensive against the Gazala Line. Although lightened, his equipment is made up from the same range of items as worn in the other main theatres of operations. His clothing owes much to pre-war Indian experience, where the normal campaign dress was khaki drill shorts, the old 'greyback' shirt, and a khaki sweater for the cool nights. During the 1930s the 'greyback' was replaced by a khaki Aertex shirt of similar colour to the KD shorts. This uniform – or Battledress, in cold weather, which was far from unknown in North Africa – was worn throughout the African campaign.

1—Mk.II steel helmet painted sand-colour.

2—Aertex cotton shirt, made of an open-weave material for coolness. Cut long, it had two pleated breast pockets, and a four-button pullover front. It was always worn open at the neck. Because shirts were washed as often as practical, insignia were not permanently attached. Chevrons of rank – in standard form, or of simple white tape – were temporarily attached either with press studs or hooks and eyes, and often to the right sleeve only. The divisional sign of the 50th Division – two Ts for 'Tyne' and 'Tees', crossed to form a rough H shape for 'Humber' – is worn on a removable shoulder strap slide.

3—1937 pattern webbing equipment; in North Africa it was scrubbed, and lengthy exposure to the sun could bleach it almost white. The combination illustrated was for personnel not issued with the rifle or light machine gun: the suspenders attach directly to the belt by means of brass and webbing connectors. The water bottle is worn behind. Our NCO has arranged his equipment to personal taste.

4—M1928 Thompson sub-machine gun, with 50-round drum magazine. Ordered in large quantities from the USA in 1940, it was the standard sub-machine gun until the general issue of the lighter, cheaper and cruder Sten gun; and was still seen in use by 8th Army units in Italy quite late in the war, since its heavy .45 calibre round and greater reliability were preferred. No item of the 1937 webbing equipment was designed to carry the large drum magazines, which were later generally discarded in favour of the box magazine which fitted into the basic pouch. This NCO has slung his 'small pack' or haversack to carry the drums. Its regulation position in fighting order was slung by shoulder straps high on the back. Its normal contents included the mess tins and eating utensils, washing and mending kit, a sweater, iron rations, and – officially, though seldom in practice – the water bottle.

5—Enfield No. 2 Mk.I .38in. revolver. This was not normally carried by junior ranks of infantry, except for medium machine gun crews. This NCO, commanding a section of ten men, is far from alone in having 'scrounged' one as a secondary weapon of last resort. He has fitted the 1937 pattern webbing holster to the bottom of the pistol cartridge pouch, and the pouch to the belt; the regulation arrangement was to fit the pouch on the left suspender, above the holster mounted on the belt, butt forwards. The pistol was retained by a neck lanyard.

6—'Shorts KD', cut very full. The waist was adjusted by two cotton straps and patent buckles. The pocket on the front held the 'first field dressing'.

7—Long socks or 'hose tops' gave some protection from sun, dust and flies.

8—Short puttees and 'anklets web' were both to be seen in the ranks of 8th Army; they gave some support to the ankle, and prevented sand getting down into the ankle boot (in theory).

9—Standard issue hobnailed 'ammunition boots'.

Philippe Charbonnier

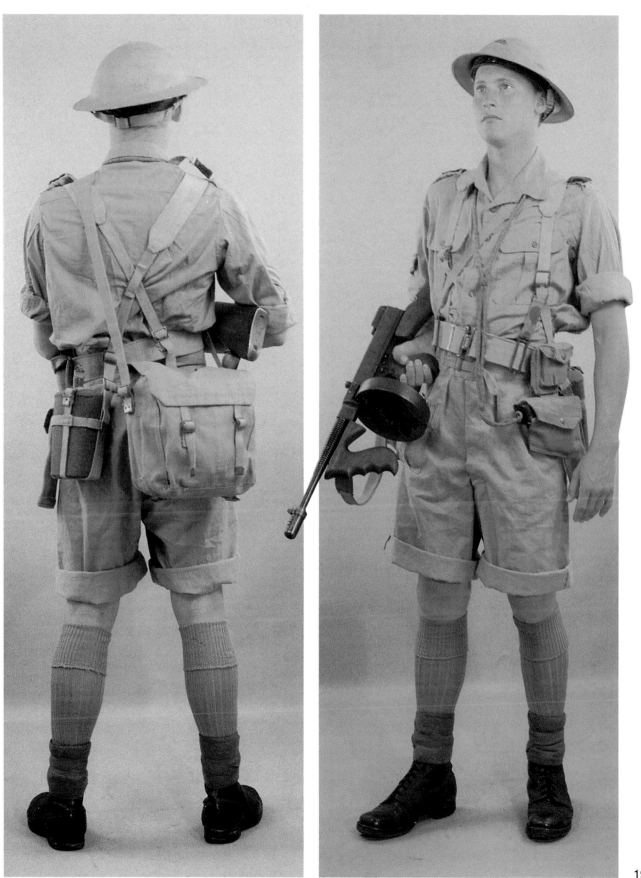

ITALIAN INFANTRYMAN, WESTERN DESERT, 1942

Italy's entry into the war in June 1940 was a gamble. Mussolini was aware of his country's lack of readiness for war against modern European enemies; but he feared that Italy would be left out of the division of spoils if Germany won a quick and easy victory, as then seemed likely. Early moves against British colonies in East Africa and threatening manoeuvres on the Libyan/Egyptian border were accompanied by an invasion of Greece. In all these campaigns large but ill-prepared Italian armies suffered almost immediate and costly set-backs at the hands of smaller enemy forces. Catastrophic reverses in Greece and North Africa forced Germany to come to her ally's aid. Large Italian forces continued to fight alongside the *Afrika Korps* throughout 1941-42; relatively short of transport and effective armour and air support, they generally provided the infantry mass, while Rommel's modern and highly mobile German divisions provided the 'punch'. The Axis defeat in North Africa in spring 1943, followed by the Allied invasion of Sicily, led to the overthrow of the Fascist government and Italy's conclusion of a unilateral armistice with the Allies in September 1943, coinciding with the Allies' invasion landings on the mainland.

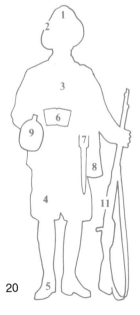

1—M1935 colonial helmet as worn by NCOs and troops. It bears the brass frontal badge of the infantry superimposed on a cockade in the national colours of red/white/green.

2—Late-model desert goggles.

3—The colonial tunic or bush-jacket called the *'sahariana'*, worn quite widely as an alternative to the lightweight khaki model of the woollen M1940 uniform. It is identifiable by the single falling collar, and by the caped effect on the chest. The collar patches are those of the 'Bologna' Division, comprising the 39th and 40th Infantry and 205th Artillery Regiments, which fought at Alamein under XXI Italian Corps.

4—The trousers, in the same light khaki cloth as the jacket, were of the same cut as the M1940 European uniform. They were gathered below the knee by laces, and confined by puttees, as often as not of European grey-green uniform cloth.

5—M1912 natural leather hobnailed boots.

6—M1907 double cartridge pouches in grey-green leather, each pocket holding four clips of 6.5mm rounds for the Carcano M1891/38 rifle or carbine. The pouch rig was standard issue on all fronts where Italian infantry fought, despite its inconvenience when the soldier had to lie down behind cover.

7—M1891 bayonet in metal scabbard, carried in a grey-green leather frog.

8—T35 gasmask in its carrier.

9—Water bottle of standard pattern, in aluminium covered with grey-green cloth, on an adjustable sling. The mouthpiece has a valve which allows a thin trickle of water to be released – theoretically, an aid to water-economy in the field, though one may doubt that it had much practical effect in the hands of troops.

10—Knapsack, stowed with the standard grey-green greatcoat and with a khaki version of the tent section. This latter was less frequently seen than the M1929 camouflaged model.

11—M1891 Carcano rifle in 6.5mm calibre.

Franco Mesturini

FRENCH FOREIGN LEGION INFANTRYMAN, WESTERN DESERT, 1942

At the time of the French Armistice in June 1940 several thousand French soldiers and sailors found themselves on British soil. Notable among these were the troops led by Gen. Béthouart, withdrawn from Norway after the Narvik campaign. They faced a crucial choice: whether to accept the Armistice and return to occupied France, and their families; or whether to fight on under the entirely new colours of the Free French, in a war whose outcome could only be guessed. Most of the *Chasseurs Alpins* and sailors chose to return home; but more than half of the Foreign Legion's *13e Demi-Brigade* elected to fight on under Gen. De Gaulle. For these *légionnaires*, voluntarily exiled from their homeland, or without any blood ties to the country of their adoption, a long and extraordinary crusade was just beginning.

From 1940 to 1943 the *légionnaires*, like the rest of the Free French forces, were supplied from British sources. The *légionnaires* made every effort to maintain their French equipment, and to keep their traditional distinctions; but actual clothing was naturally replaced fairly soon by British equivalents. From the summer of 1943, when the Free French Forces and the French Army of Africa came together after the defeat of the Axis forces in North Africa, they formed the French Army of Liberation, and were re-equipped with US uniforms, equipment and weapons.

1—The *'képi blanc'* was the distinctive headgear of the Legion. It was in fact a regulation *képi*, with a dark blue body and a crimson top, fitted with a light sun cover. Originally this had been pale khaki, but the desert sun and frequent washing bleached it white. A gold lace false chinstrap was worn by senior corporals and sergeants.

2—Another traditional item was the *'chèche'* or desert scarf, recalling old Saharan glories, and by the outbreak of war a regulation item of campaign dress for African and motorised units. As another link with their true identity it was cherished by Free French troops; it was also highly practical.

3—By the time that Gen. Koenig's 1st Free French Brigade won renown at Bir Hakeim, the Legion battalions had long since received both Battledress and tropical KD clothing from the British army. The 13e DBLE added the Free French emblem – the Cross of Lorraine – to the sleeve in red, white and blue; and Legion collar patches, of dark blue with two green pipings. The Legion's seven-flamed grenade emblem was worn on these, in green by the troops and gold by senior NCOs.

4—Old pattern French personal equipment, issued to the 13e DBLE for the Norwegian campaign, 1940, and still in use in 1942. It comprised the standard M1903/14 belt, M1892/14 suspenders, three M1916 cartridge pouches, a two-litre M1935 water bottle and sling, and a light khaki haversack used for rations and small kit.

5—British KD shorts, of the type popularly known as 'Bombay bloomers'. These could be folded down and fastened just below the knee, tucked into long socks, as protection against sun and insects and – more importantly, at the time when they were designed – blistering gas. They were hardly ever so worn, in practice.

6—British 'hose tops', often worn rolled down to the top of the boot by the French.

7—French M1917 ankle boots.

8—MAS36 rifle in 7.5mm calibre, introduced in certain infantry and all cavalry units shortly before the outbreak of war. It was issued to the Norwegian expeditionary force immediately before embarkation. The long needle-bayonet fitted into a tube beneath the barrel when not fixed, so was not carried on the belt.

Francois Vauvillier

23

ITALIAN INFANTRYMAN, ITALY, 1942

The uniform and equipment of the World War II Italian infantry did not differ markedly from those of the Great War. The uniform remained *'grigio-verde'*, the grey-green colour adopted in 1909. Successive regulations altered points of detail, but the overall appearance of the soldier hardly changed in 30 years; the only major innovation was the introduction of an open-collar tunic in 1933.

The new uniform distributed from 1940 onward was made of a half-natural, half-synthetic material, and was worn in all climates except the African desert. Personal equipment remained unchanged. As for their small arms, the Italians made a tentative effort to replace the 6.5mm calibre, proved inadequate in Ethiopia and Spain; but after going some way towards introducing new weapons in 7.35mm, they reverted to the old calibre rather than face the difficulty and expense of re-equipping an expanding army then mobilising for war. The range of infantry weapons and calibres which actually saw service proved a nightmare for the logistic services.

1—M1933 nickel-steel helmet, painted matt grey-green; it has three ventilation holes, and up to 1942 the branch- of-service badge was stencilled on the front in black.

2—M1939 shirt, of grey-green flannel for winter and lighter cloth for summer. It had a fall collar, for use with a necktie of the same shade; two buttoned breast pockets; and a two-button pullover front.

3—M1940 open-collar tunic in grey-green semi-synthetic material. It had four buttoned, patch pockets, and an integral cloth belt with two adjustment buttons. Unlike the preceding model, which had collars in various branch colours, the 1940 tunic was grey-green all over. On the sleeve is the red double chevron of a corporal, worn on both arms. The collar patches varied in colours and shape depending upon the branch of service and the formation: these white rectangles identify the 50th Division 'Regina', composed of the 9th, 10th, 309th and 331st Infantry Regiments. The silver star of Savoy was worn on all Army collar patches, by all ranks.

4—M1891 personal equipment, of leather chemically dyed greyish green. The neck suspender hooked behind the cartridge pouches; the narrow belt was worn with the buckle offset to the left.

5—M1907 double cartridge pouches, each pocket holding four clips of 6.5mm Carcano ammunition.

6—Standard issue water bottle in cloth-covered aluminium; one- and two-litre sizes were issued according to branch of service.

7—M1939 knapsack in heavy canvas with leather straps. It had three interior compartments; and the external straps allowed stowage of a rolled greatcoat, blanket, and M1929 camouflaged tent section, the latter also serving as a poncho.

8—M1933 gasmask satchel, used as a haversack for small kit since the introduction of the T35 gasmask.

9—Mess tin, made in aluminium since 1930. Of oval shape, it could be carried either strapped to the haversack, or, as here, in its own cover.

10—M1891 bayonet frog, linked to the entrenching tool carrier. This latter could accommodate several different tools – here, a shovel.

11—Grey-green uniform trousers of foot troops' pattern, reaching below the knee, where they are confined by puttees.

12—M1912 natural leather hobnailed boots.

13—M1941 Carcano rifle in 6.5mm calibre – a slightly modified development of the old M1891.

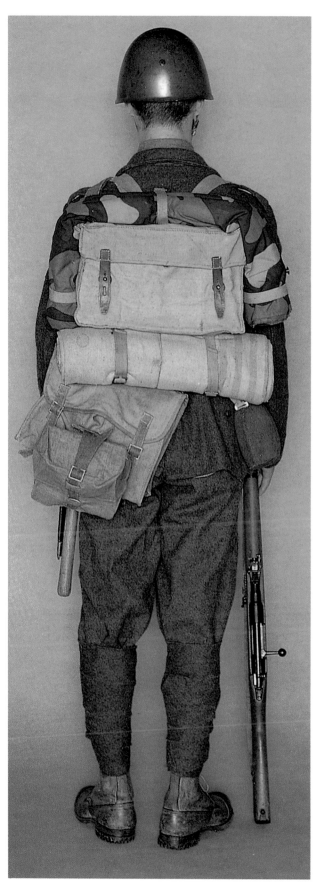

SOVIET INFANTRYMAN, WINTER 1941

The uniforms of the Soviet Army underwent a radical process of reform in the years following 1918, when a conscious effort was made to turn away from the long Imperial tradition. In 1936 a new, predominantly khaki uniform was adopted; though generally of a modern and practical cut, it had certain short-comings which were shown up by the Russo-Finnish campaign of 1939. This 'Winter War' cost thousands of Soviet lives through the failure to provide adequate protection against the cold, which often fell to 40° below zero. An efficient cold-weather garment, the *'telogreika'*, was later mass-produced. The first issues of this uniform proved their worth in the savage winter of 1941/42, when the German *Wehrmacht's* lightning drive into the heart of European Russia was halted before Moscow; German troops, dressed only in the woollen uniforms suitable for a temperate winter, faced Soviet reinforcements trained, and suitably equipped, in Siberia.

1—M1940 *'shapka-ushanka'* cap in fleece-trimmed cloth, which replaced the pointed cloth *'budionovka'* bonnet of the Russian Civil War. The *'ushanka'* was popular, and efficient; it was even seen worn under the steel helmet, and was copied by the German *Wehrmacht* and later by many other armies. The officers' version had real fur trim, the troops' artificial fur (popularly known as 'fish fur'!)

2—Enamelled red star badge; a plainer khaki-painted version was also used.

3—The *'telogreika'* jacket M1941, in quilted khaki cloth. At this date it was not generally available, and was much sought after. Its simple, capacious design was highly efficient for field wear in the coldest climates. Manufactured – like most Soviet uniform items – at factories dispersed over a huge country disrupted by war, it appeared with a number of slightly varying designs of pockets, buttons, collar and wrist tabs, etc.

4—Trousers, made in the same quilted material as the jacket. These were rather less often seen than the jacket, perhaps because some soldiers found them encumbering. There were wide colour variations between jackets and trousers, across the whole range of khakis from yellow-brown to green-brown.

5—Standard belt in natural leather, with a single-prong buckle; the belt was virtually unchanged since before the Revolution.

6—Holster for the Nagant M1895 7.62mm revolver. Although completely out of date by 1941 this was still on issue to many officers and some NCOs, and to certain categories of soldiers – signallers, machine gunners, drivers, etc. It was slowly replaced by the Tokarev TT33 of the same calibre, which was first issued during the Russo-Finnish War.

7—Map case in natural leather issued to officers, NCO section commanders and reconnaissance personnel; there were many variations of material and detail design.

8—Black leather boots, traditional to the Russian soldier for more than a century. In very cold weather they were often replaced by loose felt *'valenki'*, which could be stuffed with insulating material.

9—Carrier for the drum magazine of the PPSh41 sub-machine gun, in heavy khaki canvas.

10—PPSh41 sub-machine gun, designed by the engineer Shpagin and suitable for mass-production methods. This robust, reliable weapon became the 'trademark' of the Soviet soldier; although supplies only allowed its issue to the pick of front line troops in 1941, some five million were made during the war, and it – or the later PPD43 sub-machine gun – became the personal weapon of about one Red Army infantryman in every three. It fired standard 7.62mm ammunition, and the drum accommodated 71 rounds. The combination of short accurate range and high rate of fire accorded with the aggressive combat doctrine encouraged by the Soviets.

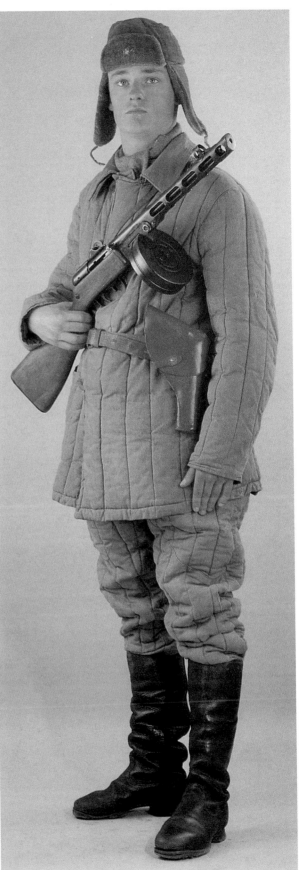

GERMAN LIGHT MACHINE GUNNER, RUSSIAN FRONT, SUMMER 1943

After four years of war the outline of the German front-line infantryman had undergone a noticeable change. The basic uniforms and equipment were still those of 1939; but there now appeared the first sizeable issues of camouflage-cloth combat smocks and helmet covers, following the example offered by the troops of *Waffen-SS* formations since 1938. The equipment actually carried in the assault was lighter than ever: the mobile German infantryman was able to leave much of his kit in his truck or halftrack transporter during actual combat. The soldier illustrated is a light machine gunner, and carries on his person all necessary special equipment for this function. Each infantry section had at least one LMG.

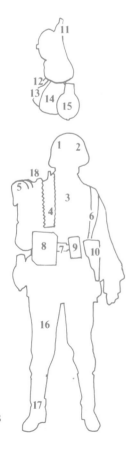

1—M1942 steel helmet, a simplified version of the M1935: to ease mass production the edge was left 'raw', and turned outwards, instead of being turned under all round like the 1935 helmet.

2—Improvised camouflage net. Helmet covers made in the angular three-colour 'splinter' camouflage pattern used by the Army (as opposed to *Waffen-SS*) also appeared in 1942/43.

3—Camouflage smock; this shows in clear detail the 'splinter' pattern, first adopted for the *Zeltbahn* shelter half/tent section as early as 1931. The smock was of loose cut, tightened by elasticated laces at wrists, neck and waist, and with vertical slits allowing access to the pockets of the woollen uniform worn under the smock.

4—Belt of 150 7.92mm cartridges, made of metal links.

5—M1934 drum magazine, with a capacity of 50 rounds, used on the weapon for assaults and other occasions when the belt would be inconvenient. Pairs of drums could be carried in a special container.

6—M1939 infantry equipment suspenders, in leather with matt grey metal fixtures; normally engaged with the rifleman's cartridge pouches, they could also fix to the alternative items carried on the front of the belt, as here.

7—Black leather belt, with the Army's grey-painted buckle plate bearing the traditional Prussian motto 'God With Us' around the endorsed-wing eagle and swastika emblem.

8—Accessory pouch for the MG34 light machine gun: it contains an anti-aircraft sight, an extractor tool, an oil can, a spare breechblock, a belt feeder tongue, a flash-hider, a protective glove for changing hot barrels, and various maintenance and cleaning tools.

9—Standard issue pocket flashlight.

10—Pistol holster, as issued to machine gunners for personal sidearms – here, the Walther P38 9mm automatic.

11—'Assault pack' or webbing frame, hooked to the D-rings of the equipment suspenders and looped to the belt. Its straps allowed stowage of minimal assault equipment: the mess tin, the *Zeltbahn*, and a bag containing iron rations, tent pegs, etc.

12—M1938 gasmask in black rubber, carried in its painted metal canister, here of the second type.

13—Satchel for the proofed anti-gas cape, normally carried strapped to the gasmask canister although this was officially forbidden.

14—M1931 'breadbag' haversack, containing small personal items, field cap, rations, etc. It was carried looped to the belt.

15—M1931 water bottle, of enamelled metal painted olive.

16—Field grey cloth trousers, of straight cut; these were unchanged since the beginning of the war, apart from the abandonment of the 'stone grey' shade originally seen.

17—Black leather marching boots, or 'dice shakers', their height slightly reduced at the end of 1939.

18—*Leichter Maschinengewehr MG34*, the basic automatic weapon of the infantry section. This should properly be termed a 'general purpose' machine gun; it was more sophisticated and much faster-firing than the magazine-fed LMGs of Allied armies, and when fitted to a tripod mount could perform all the fixed-firing tasks of a medium machine gun.

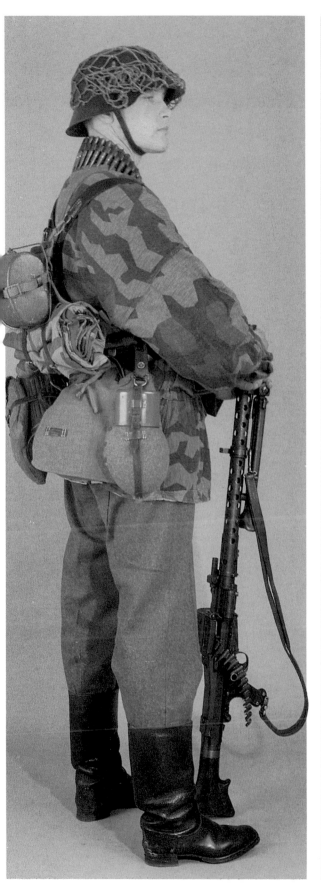

SOVIET INFANTRYMAN, SUMMER 1943

On 15 January 1943 Stalin signed the regulations known as *'Prikaz 25'* of the National Defence Commissariat, which detailed, in 64 pages, the new uniforms of the Red Army. This document marked an astonishing about-face, in that it revived significant traditional uniform features which had been suppressed since the Revolution. While most noticeable in the case of officers' uniforms, these 'folk-lore' items (high collar, shoulder straps, etc.) extended to all ranks. At a time of low morale, after suffering repeated defeats and millions of casualties, the Soviet regime consciously summoned up the ancient patriotic spirit of the Motherland; and any reminders of even Tsarist glory were pressed into service. The revived prestige of the soldier's uniform had a positive effect on the morale of the *'Frontovik'*.

1—M1935 *'pilotka'* cap; this khaki sidecap, worn tilted to the right, was the everyday headgear of the Soviet ranker in temperate weather. All enlisted ranks wore the red enamelled star badge, or its field quality equivalent in khaki-painted metal.

2—The traditional *'gymnastiorka'* shirt-tunic of the Russian soldier, M1943. The standard garment of the soldier in temperate weather, this khaki cotton item had a stand collar closed by two small buttons. This soldier displays the Medal of Military Valour: in the traditional Russian style, medals were worn even in combat.

3—M1943 shoulder boards. These were of khaki cloth, with a piping in branch-of-service colour (raspberry red for infantry, or more properly, 'rifles') and NCOs' rank insignia in the form of red stripes of varying numbers and widths. Officers had parade shoulder boards in metallic lace, as well as a subdued field version.

4—Standard issue belt.

5—M1930 cartridge pouches, the two pockets each containing three five-round clips of 7.62mm ammunition for the rifle.

6—M1940 helmet, which replaced the M1936 type distinguished by an appliqué metal crest. Of very modern form, this helmet is still in widespread use today.

7—Khaki cloth satchel for the new BN gasmask.

8—M1935 *'sharovari'* trousers of khaki cotton cloth. All branches wore the same half-breeches; note the characteristic pointed reinforcement patches on the knees.

9—Standard issue black leather boots.

10—M1939 knapsack; it gradually replaced the old pack called a *'meshok'*, but the latter was still seen in large numbers. The M1939 pack was of khaki cloth with leather edging and straps, though wartime economy sometimes replaced these fixtures with cloth equivalents. The shoulder straps hooked to rings behind the cartridge pouches at the front.

11—Khaki *'plashch-palatka'* tent section, which could be used as a hooded rain cape by manipulation of cords and slots; it was worn over all personal equipment. The greatcoat could also be worn rolled in a 'horseshoe'.

12—Square-headed entrenching tool in its canvas carrier; there were many slightly varying types in simultaneous use.

13—Aluminium water bottle carried in a khaki cloth pocket fastened by press studs.

14—M1891/30 Mosin Nagant 7.62mm rifle. The 1930 variant of a line of weapons stretching back to the last century was modelled on the 1891 dragoon model, shorter than the contemporary infantry rifle. It stayed in service right up to the end of World War II despite being seriously outclassed by more modern designs. Many Soviet soldiers received either the PPSh41 sub-machine gun, or the semi-automatic Tokarev SVT40 rifle. The old Mosin Nagant was provided with a hiltless cruciform needle bayonet, but seldom with a scabbard: if the bayonet was issued it was carried fixed at all times.

WAFFEN-SS INFANTRYMAN, RUSSIAN FRONT, SUMMER 1943

Raised from the pre-war paramilitary SS militia, the *Waffen-SS* evolved during the war years into what was almost a 'parallel army', many hundreds of thousands strong and organised into more than 30 divisions – some of them the largest, best-equipped, and most formidable combat formations in the *Wehrmacht*. From a low initial reputation among the professionals of the *Heer*, they rose to become the ever-reliable 'fire brigade', committed as the spearhead of attack or the last line of hopeless defence. Their field grey uniforms were generally identical to those of the Army apart from their special insignia; and their personal equipment and weapons – although initially drawn from obsolete stocks – were by 1941 standard current *Wehrmacht* issue.

1—M1935 steel helmet. The characteristic W-SS camouflage cover, which was worn from the first days of World War II, was made from no less than 14 separate pieces of cloth; and fixed by an 'envelope' which slipped under the front brim, and three spring hooks which engaged at sides and rear. Like all the many patterns of camouflage smock, the helmet covers were reversible, the colours being predominantly brown on one side for autumn and winter, and predominantly green on the other for spring and summer. This is an early cover, lacking the later external loops for foliage.

2—Only the collar of the tunic is seen above the camouflage smock. It bears the black collar patches of the W-SS: on the right, bearing the SS runes badge of the whole organisation, and on the left bearing a system of rank insignia peculiar to the SS, here the two stripes of a corporal; both collar insignia were embroidered in white or silver-grey for enlisted ranks.

3—Camouflage smock, first tested by the W-SS as early as 1938, and later issued universally to all combat personnel. It was copied by the rest of the *Wehrmacht* in various ways; and, since World War II, by almost every army in the world – it was a genuinely important innovation in military dress. Of loose cut, gathered at wrist, waist and neck by elastics or laces, it was worn over the woollen uniform but under the equipment. This is a model manufactured in 1942-44, with two skirt pockets; earlier smocks had only vertical slits through which the uniform pockets could be reached. Another sign of a late-pattern smock is the series of loops sewn onto the shoulders and arms, for attaching foliage. There were about seven variations of camouflage pattern, in light and dark greens, light and dark browns, even orange and violet shades; all featured small, basically rounded patches of superimposed colours in patterns resembling leaves. Here both smock and helmet cover display the 'spring/summer' side.

4—M1939 black leather infantry equipment suspenders.

5—Standard issue black leather rifle cartridge pouches, two sets of three, holding a total of 12 five-round clips of 7.92mm Mauser ammunition.

6—M1924 hand grenade.

7—Standard issue black leather belt, the buckle plate of grey-painted metal bearing a design peculiar to the SS: an eagle with outstretched wings, clutching a swastika, the wings breaking a riband bearing the motto 'My Honour Is Loyalty'.

8—M1884/98 bayonet in old-pattern black leather frog (lacking a hilt strap).

9—Folding entrenching shovel, in its metal-reinforced leather carrier, which included a fitment to hold steady the bayonet scabbard.

10—M1938 gasmask in its painted metal canister.

11—Anti-gas cape, here in a late type of satchel made in ordinary (i.e. non-proofed) cloth.

12—Reversible camouflaged *Zeltbahn* in W-SS pattern, here simply strapped to the belt – a common practice when in lightened assault harness.

13—M1931 water bottle, with tinned, olive-painted cup.

14—M1931 'breadbag'.

15—M1942 trousers in field grey cloth. These had belt-loops; and tightening laces and instep straps at the bottom of each leg, introduced for use with ankle boots and web anklets, which replaced the old high 'dice shakers' in the middle war years.

16—Canvas anklets, with leather straps.

17—Ankle boots in natural leather, first issued to some troops in 1937, replaced the high boots during the war years for economy reasons. Usually blacked in use, they sometimes appeared in natural tan.

18—Mauser 98k 7.92mm rifle.

33

JAPANESE INFANTRYMAN, SUMMER 1942

At the time of Japan's entry into the war on 7 December 1941, the Japanese infantryman was equipped with an outfit which had benefitted from prolonged field experience in Manchuria and China. In 1941-42 the infantryman wore the Model 98 uniform, introduced in 1938. This was made in both khaki-brown cloth for winter and lighter cotton for summer and tropical use. The *Hetai*, as the Emperor's footslogger was known, confronted the Allied forces in the Pacific theatre in this simple uniform; and the model illustrated here wears summer dress with complete marching kit. In accordance with tradition he carries a flag presented to him by his family.

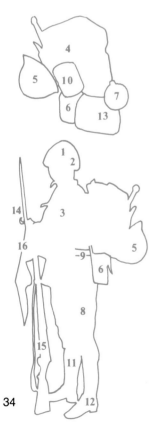

1—Model 92 (1932) helmet, adopted during the Chinese campaign; the pot-shaped steel shell, painted khaki-brown, was fitted to the head by small adjustable pads inside. The frontal insignia was in the form of a star for the Army and an anchor for Marines.

2—A helmet cover was often worn laced in place, in khaki quilted linen, with a yellow star or anchor badge sewn onto a round piece of uniform cloth.

3—Tunic Model 98 (1938), in cotton for tropical wear. It has five front buttons, two hip vents, a tab to support the belt on the left where the bayonet was slung, and four buttoned pockets. Collar patches bore the insignia of rank, here those of a private first class.

4—Rectangular canvas knapsack, with cloth stowage straps retaining the exterior load, which here includes a waterproof rolled inside the tent section (which could be worn as a poncho), spare boots, and the entrenching spade, its head removed from the haft and carried in a cloth cover.

5—Tropical helmet. There were a number of different types; this one is made of cork with a cotton cover. There was also a flexible version, which the soldier could wear under his steel helmet.

6—Gasmask, similar in design to the British box respirator.

7—M1933 water bottle, in khaki-painted aluminium. A strap of the carrier passed through the ring on the stopper.

8—Trousers, loosely cut in 'half-breeches' shape from khaki cotton. They were gathered at the ankle by means of buttons, laces or press-studs.

9—Natural leather belt with a single-prong buckle. The three cartridge pouches fastened with straps and studs. The front pair held 30 rounds each; the larger, rear pouch held 60 rounds and the rifle cleaning kit. The bayonet frog, also in natural tan leather, was worn on the left.

10—Mess tin in khaki-painted aluminium, strapped to the pack.

11—Khaki puttees were made of either winter or summer weight uniform cloth; note the 'X'-effect of the pattern, characteristic of the Japanese.

12—Standard issue army boots in natural leather.

13—Cloth haversack for personal effects.

14—Quillon bayonet for the Model 38 Arisaka rifle.

15—Model 38 rifle, named after its inventor, Col. Nariaki Arisaska. In service with the Japanese Army from 1906 to 1945, this was a 6.5mm weapon which appeared in both 'long' and 'short' models – though at 44ins., even the 'short' type was unwieldy enough for short Japanese soldiers in thick jungle.

16—The *'Buun-Tchokyu'*, a patriotic good-luck flag inscribed by the soldier's family and friends with prayers for honour and good fortune.

US MARINE INFANTRYMAN, MARIANA ISLANDS, JUNE 1944

The crack infantry of the US Marine Corps were linked administratively to the US Navy rather than the Army. Their tactical employment, and details of their clothing and equipment, also distinguished them from the bulk of America's foot-soldiers. They specialised in amphibious assault, and were employed almost exclusively in the Pacific theatre of operations. During the savage and costly 'island-hopping' counteroffensive against the Japanese, which lasted three and a half years, they became renowned for their fighting qualities and their tenacity, at a heavy cost in lives. Our subject here is a sniper from the 2nd Marine Division. The Japanese were adept at last-ditch defence of cunningly concealed positions, and their snipers held up many advances; the Marines were obliged to put much effort into locating and neutralising them.

1—Standard M1 steel helmet, here with the cloth camouflage cover peculiar to the US Marines; like other camouflaged uniform items, it was predominantly brown and beige on one side, and predominantly green on the other, being theoretically reversible for operations on beaches or in jungle. In practice, this did not make much difference. The cover was occasionally stencilled in black with the USMC's eagle, globe and anchor badge. The olive drab fatigue cap was often worn under the helmet; it, too, often bore the Corps badge.

2—M1941 fatigue jacket, in herringbone cotton twill, also in what was officially called 'olive drab' but which quickly faded in use to a pale grey-green. It has three patch pockets without flaps, the USMC acronym and emblem being stencilled on the left breast pocket. The front and cuffs are fastened with brass buttons. The marine's identity discs or 'dog tags' are slung round his neck on a lace.

3—Ammunition bandolier, a throw-away item issued already packed with 12 clips for the rifle.

4—The US Marine M1941 Pack System consisted of a knapsack, which could be worn alone, and a haversack, which could be attached below the knapsack, the combination being known as the 'transport pack'. The T-handled entrenching spade is attached here to the flap of the knapsack. The shelter half/poncho, in US Marine camouflage material, is rolled up and strapped round the knapsack.

5—War booty: a Japanese water bottle and flag. Such souvenirs were prized, and could be traded with rear-echelon personnel for cash, drink, or other comforts.

6—M4 satchel for the M6 gasmask, an Army issue item.

7—'Jungle first aid pouch' hooked to the belt; the standard first aid pouch is hooked below it.

8—M1941 fatigue trousers, in the same material as the jacket; they had two slanted front pockets and two patch rear pockets, the buttons being the same design as those on the jacket.

9—USMC web leggings, which had fewer eyelets than the standard issue type. In the Pacific the trousers were often worn loose or rolled.

10—Standard issue boots of natural leather, 'rough side out', with rubber heels and soles.

11—Rifle belt M1918/23 of webbing, consisting of ten pouches with snap studs, each containing two clips of .30 calibre cartridges. The equipment suspenders attached to the belt eyelets with snap hooks, and crossed in the middle of the back. A hand grenade, Mk.II defensive, is carried with its lever hooked through the D-ring of one suspender. The water bottle in its fabric carrier, and a leather-sheathed fighting knife, are also hooked to the lower eyelets.

12—Springfield M1903 A4 rifle, with telescopic sights. The old bolt-action Springfield was preferred, over the semi-automatic Garand M1 which armed most riflemen, for sniping work: rate of fire was less important than accuracy.

JAPANESE INFANTRYMAN, SPRING 1944

The simple, lightweight Japanese uniform was from the first quite suitable for tropical campaigning, and underwent little change during the war years. As wartime shortages began to bite there was a certain amount of substitution of non-strategic materials, however: many leather items were replaced with cheaper equivalents made of vulcanised fibre or rubberised cloth.

This soldier is wearing the lightened equipment typical of the jungle campaigns. The cap, shirt, and 'horseshoe roll' containing basic necessities were characteristic of the defenders of the Pacific Islands against the US forces, and of Burma against the British 14th Army. Although some issue items – e.g. the gasmask – have been discarded as useless encumbrances, he still carries, fixed to his bayonet, the good-luck flag presented by his family.

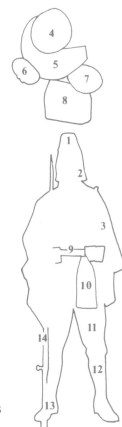

1—Campaign cap in light cloth, introduced in 1938; manufactured in various materials, it was the most characteristic headgear of the Japanese soldier. It always bore on the front either the yellow star of the Army or the anchor of the Imperial Marines. The example illustrated has an 'economy' chinstrap, and tightens at the rear by means of a lace.

2—Neck flap, hooked to the cap for tropical campaigning; it is made from four rectangles of cloth.

3—Cotton shirt, normally worn under a tunic, but worn alone in hot climates; it buttons all the way down the front, and has two breast pockets. Rank insignia were fixed above the left pocket – here, that of a private first class.

4—Model 1932 steel helmet, with its quilted cloth sun-cover (which also bears the yellow star badge). The helmet was often worn on top of the fatigue cap.

5—'Horseshoe roll' of spare clothes and basic necessities: a less encumbering way of carrying equipment than the issue knapsack, and one adopted by many armies over the centuries. It could be made with the tent section, or a purpose-made holdall.

6—Mess tin of khaki-painted aluminium, strapped to the equipment roll.

7—Final model water bottle, in khaki-painted aluminium, in its slung carrier.

8—Light canvas haversack, containing the bare minimum of personal items, washing kit, eating utensils, minimal rations, etc.

9—The soldier has kept his leather belt, but his ammunition pouches are made of vulcanised fibre, typical of the latter part of the war; fabric belts were also common.

10—This cloth bag, marked with ideograms, contains the soldier's most valued possessions and his personal documents.

11—Cotton 'half-breeches', gathered at the ankle by buttons or laces. The outline of these trousers varied, from something resembling jodhpurs to a straighter 'plus-fours' shape.

12—Puttees, of either heavy wool or light cotton cloth, held in placed by the characteristically Japanese cross-gartered tapes.

13—Standard issue natural leather boots; in the tropics these were often replaced by 'jikatabi', campaign shoes of fabric and rubber, with a separated big toe.

14—Model 38 Arisaka rifle – the number referring to the 38th year of the Emperor Meiji's dynasty or 1906. There was an attempt to replace this outdated 6.5mm calibre weapon with the newer Model 99 in the 7.7mm calibre already employed by the Model 92 machine gun; but it was never completed, and the confusion of calibres made for logistic difficulties.

US ARMY INFANTRY NCO, PHILIPPINES, MAY 1945

Undistinguished by any give-away mark of his rank which might draw sniper fire, this NCO is dressed like the majority of the US Army infantry fighting in the Pacific in the closing months of the war. The special demands on uniform and equipment made by campaigning in the tropics were the subject of extensive technical studies. After the limited issue of camouflage uniforms, the Army reverted to a less conspicuous and more comfortable green fatigue outfit.

1—M1 steel helmet; the main chinstrap was often left hanging unfastened in action, with the narrow leather strap of the liner up over the brim.

2—M1943 fatigue jacket; originally a working and training uniform, these fatigues quickly became the standard combat clothing for the tropics. The jacket is made of cotton herringbone twill, and is identifiable by the large breast pockets, originally designed to take a ration pack. It is unlined, and was often worn hanging loose over the trousers. The buttons were of black metal, or sometimes of plastic; the straight cuffs had two alternative buttons for adjusting the fit.

3—M1 carbine with 15-round magazine. This weapon was originally designed to replace the M1911A1 automatic pistol as the personal arm of service troops and junior leaders, but many personnel were attracted by its lightness and handiness. In practice, it was found to lack stopping-power: note that our sergeant has also kept the M1911A1 Colt .45 automatic, in its M1916 holster – the big .45 rounds had much greater impact than the carbine's .30 calibre ammunition – and an M3 fighting knife. A double magazine pouch for the carbine is fixed to the weapon's butt.

4—M3 binoculars, 6x30; the M1917 leather case could be carried on its sling, or looped to the belt.

5—Webbing equipment. The M1936 pistol belt carries, from left to right: M1910 water bottle, pistol holster, double magazine pouch for the pistol, jungle first aid pack with M1942 first aid dressing pouch attached. On the back, an M1936 musette (general purpose haversack) is carried slung by the universal carrying strap, and contains rations and small personal kit. A second water bottle is hooked to the rear of the belt; and the proofed tent section-cum-poncho is folded over the belt.

6—M1943 fatigue trousers, with large thigh pockets. Note the faded colour, due to prolonged exposure to sun, and washing.

7—Jungle boots, made of leather and canvas, inspired by the all-leather double-buckle combat boot M1943 which appeared in the ranks in 1944. These jungle boots, which had moulded rubber soles, first reached the troops in the last months of the war. They replaced the earlier issue leather ankle boots, and the web leggings (which most troops in the Pacific tended to discard anyway, rolling their trouser legs above the ankle boots for coolness and easy drainage).

Philippe Charbonnier

FRENCH INFANTRYMAN,
VICHY ZONE OF FRANCE, SUMMER 1942

After the Armistice of June 1940 the new Vichy government was permitted to retain a small army for maintaining internal order and protecting overseas colonial territories. The bulk of this force were still uniformed as they had been in 1939-40; but a new uniform, 'model 1941', began to be manufactured and issued in summer 1942.

In November 1942, after the Allied landings in French North Africa and the German occupation of the French 'Free Zone', the Army of the Armistice inside France was disbanded; and France's African garrisons rallied to the Allies, forming the core of the Army of Liberation. The M1941 uniform continued to be made during 1943-44, and was distributed to various personnel, including the so-called '1st Regiment of France'; the *Milice* (who received dark blue versions intended for the *Chasseurs à Pied*, as well as the standard khaki version); and also, by the Free French authorities in autumn 1944, to the *Maquis* units and the reformed regiments which were put into the line alongside the Allies in the last winter of the war.

1—Steel helmet M1926, with M1937 frontal emblem on a metal disc. The new 1941 system had been intended to include a helmet with a small metal crest and a front buffer, like those of French motorised troops, but it never appeared.

2—M1941 shirt and tie. The shirt differed from the M1935 type mainly in having shoulder straps; the tie was of tapered shape, ending in a point, whereas the old tie had been straight and square-ended.

3—M1941 tunic. Originally this had been intended only for a walking-out and parade dress, and a heavy canvas jacket – modelled on those used by the ski-troops in the Norwegian campaign of 1940 – had been planned for field wear. In practice the latter never appeared, so the tunic had to do service as an all-purpose uniform. Its shape recalled that of the previous uniform for officers, with an open collar and four pockets; removable 'rolled' shoulder straps were added for campaign use, and the cuffs were buttoned to allow them to be turned up. The citation lanyard in the red of the *Légion d'Honneur* was worn by the 1st Infantry, whose patch this man wears, with the cipher and pipings in the new colour – crimson – of the 1942 issue uniform.

4—M1935 equipment, unchanged since 1939-40. No gasmask is carried: its issue was forbidden under the terms of the Franco-German Armistice.

5—M1941 trousers, of straight cut; they were designed to be worn loose at the ankle in walking-out dress. The cloth, of the same khaki shade as the tunic, was of inferior quality, and tended to turn greyish with use.

6—M1941 half-gaiters. Some issue of front-lacing gaiters had been made to the infantry in spring 1940, replacing the old puttees. The 1941 model were more rigid, with side fastenings and a 'spat' section covering the top of the boot.

7—M1941 boots, of a new design with a hardened, rounded toe.

8—MAS36 rifle; enough remained after the Armistice to equip the whole Vichy army, which had slightly less than 100,000 men.

Francois Vauvillier

BRITISH BREN GUNNER, SICILY, JULY 1943

After the final victory in North Africa in May 1943, the British 8th Army landed in Sicily as a necessary prelude to an invasion of the Italian mainland. Montgomery's desert veterans, drawn from many Commonwealth nations and fighting alongside French, Polish and Canadian comrades as well as the US 5th Army, now faced a slow, costly, two-year campaign against stubborn, skilled German defenders of a series of strong natural positions.

In summer the climate and terrain differed little from that encountered in the last stages of the African campaign, and the 8th Army retained their desert uniforms. The substitution of full-length trousers in khaki drill for the desert shorts was the only major change to the infantryman's silhouette. In the extremely cold, wet Italian mountain winters Battledress was issued, and proved barely adequate in conditions as bad as anything suffered by the 2nd Army in North-West Europe.

1—Mk.II steel helmet, finished with matt paint, and covered with a camouflage net. Photographs show that hessian and/or foliage 'garnish' was applied to this sparingly, if at all, in the Italian theatre.

2—The 'Aertex' cotton shirt in pale khaki, as worn in Africa.

3—Woollen V-neck pullover in khaki. This was issued in all theatres, and was a useful and comfortable field garment in weather too warm for regular use of the Battledress blouse.

4—1937 pattern webbing equipment, in 'Field Service Marching Order' arrangement. The haversack or 'small pack' worn on the back in 'Battle Order' (not worn here) usually moved to the left hip, where it was attached to the suspender/brace ends; and the 'large pack' or valise – an item retained from the old '08 pattern equipment – was worn on the back instead. It was attached by means of the same removable L-shaped straps as the small pack in this position; the hooks at the angle of the 'L' engaged with the buckles of the universal pouches. The valise contained changes of underwear, shirt, socks, etc., spare boots, canvas and rubber 'plimsolls', and personal kit; washing kit, towel, groundsheet/rain cape, and other necessities were divided between large and small packs when both were carried. In actual combat the valise was left with the unit transport, together with greatcoats and blankets if they were not immediately needed. The bayonet was not compatible with a light machine gun, but in fact was used on campaign mainly for 'camp chores' or for mine-probing, and was sometimes retained by Bren gunners. Note the issue jackknife.

5—Water bottle, unchanged since the 1908 equipment. There were two types of carrier, one a complete 'pocket' and the other in open strapwork. The bottle had been intended to be carried in the small pack, but the addition of extra items of kit to the soldier's load meant that it was almost invariably moved to the belt to make room in the haversack.

6—Entrenching tool, its steel mattock head carried in the webbing pocket and its haft buckled across the outside.

7—Khaki drill full length tropical trousers, which began to be issued to all troops in this theatre. They were modelled on the Battledress trousers in that they too had the large (left thigh) map pocket and small (right hip) first field dressing pocket.

8—Bren Mk.I light machine gun, .303in. calibre. This was the infantry section's main firepower, and each ten-man section consisted of a two-man Bren group led by the lance-corporal deputy section leader, and six riflemen led by the corporal section leader. Simple, robust, very reliable, and extremely accurate at normal battle ranges, the Bren was a popular weapon. Its 30-round curved box magazines were carried in the universal pouches; the Bren 'No.1' carried four, his 'No.2' four, and the lance-corporal four. Each rifleman also carried two magazines, and these could be passed to the Bren group as needed.

9—'Anklets web', the short buckled gaiters worn by most British troops of all branches of service.

10 — Standard issue hobnailed 'ammunition boots'.

Philippe Charbonnier

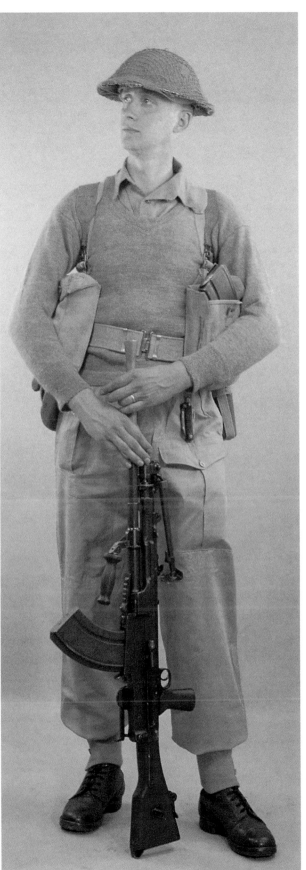

45

ITALIAN 'BERSAGLIERI' INFANTRYMAN, ITALIAN SOCIAL REPUBLIC, 1944

On 15 September 1943 the Italian Social Republic was created: a puppet Fascist mini-state in the territory still occupied by German troops, and nominally ruled by Mussolini, who had been rescued from his pro-Allied captors by Otto Skorzeny's daring commando raid. The army of the RSI was made up of Italian Fascists still loyal to Mussolini, drawn from the ranks of the old royal army and the Blackshirt militia. Four divisions strong, this force was largely formed and trained in Germany.

At first the RSI troops wore the uniforms of the old royal army with the addition of new insignia, the Roman sword being a common emblem. But despite their unenviable military situation and threatening future, the RSI soon produced quite a range of new outfits which, together with a mixture of old uniforms, camouflage garments and German items, gave the Fascist troops a characteristic appearance. The soldier illustrated is a senior corporal ('corporal-major') of *Bersaglieri* light infantry in the newly formed 'Italia' Division.

1—M1933 steel helmet; unchanged in form, it is here garnished with camouflage, a tricolour insignia, and the black cock's feather plume traditional to *Bersaglieri*.

2—M1939 grey-green flannel shirt.

3—M1940 anorak, in grey-brown windproof material. Originally peculiar to *Alpini* and *Bersaglieri*, this garment was more widely distributed late in the war. It has a fall collar, four buttoned pockets, and six front buttons. The crimson 'flame' collar insignia traditional to the *Bersaglieri* bear the Roman sword and wreath of the RSI in place of the star of the old royal army. The red and gold chevron insignia of corporal-major are sewn above the left breast pocket; above the right pocket is the badge worn by RSI soldiers whose units had been trained and formed in Germany. Below the rank insignia is an RSI volunteers' badge, with the unofficial death's-head badge popular among Mussolini's last fanatics.

4—Bayonet/dagger for the MAB38a sub-machine gun, with a folding blade, and a hilt-hook which kept it at this tilted angle on the belt.

5—M1944 belt, an obvious copy of the German type, the buckle plate bearing an eagle and *fasces* emblem.

6—Magazine pouches, also copied from German models; the body was made of canvas, with leather flaps and straps. Each pouch carried three box magazines. The suspender is the old M1891 type – a good example of the mixture of old and new in RSI equipment.

7—M1939 rectangular knapsack, with the blanket and camouflaged tent section/poncho rolled and strapped to it.

8—M1941 trousers; taken from Italian army paratrooper stocks, these grey-green trousers were cut straight, and fastened at the ankle with buttoned tabs or laces. They are tucked into the socks in this photograph; they were often worn without any sort of puttees or gaiters. The paratrooper trousers had two oblique side pockets and two buttoned rear 'revolver pockets'.

9—Standard issue black leather M1912 boots.

10—Standard issue one-litre aluminium canteen with cloth cover.

11—Beretta M1938a sub-machine gun – an excellent weapon, prized by any Allied soldier who could lay hands on one. It has two triggers, the front one for single shots and the rear one for bursts. A special cartridge (9mm 38a) was issued for this weapon, but it would also take the Glisenti 9mm and German Parabellum 9mm rounds. Widely used on all fronts by Italian troops, and distributed in large numbers to the RSI forces, it was actually put back into production, after a six-year interval, in 1950.

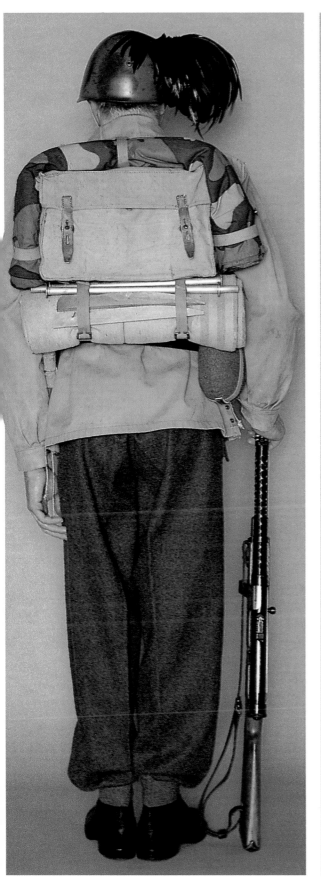
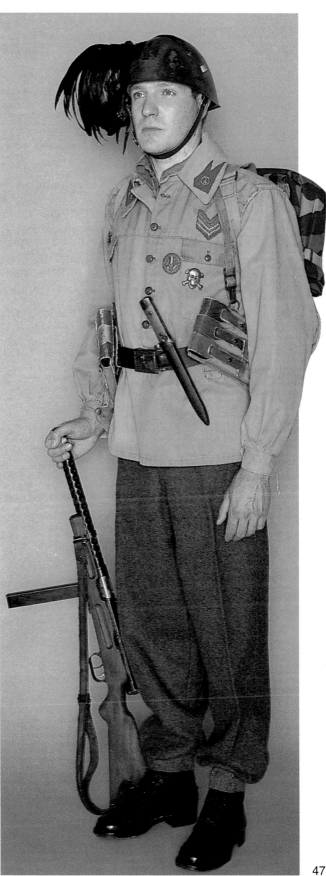

47

GERMAN MOUNTAIN INFANTRYMAN, ITALIAN FRONT, SUMMER 1944

Thanks to an intelligent use of limited manpower and resources, in a terrain which greatly favoured the defence over the attack, the German troops in Italy managed to delay the Allies right up until the end of the war in 1945 – a final defeat suffered on other fronts, which found significant German forces still in place on the southern frontiers of the Reich. Although stripped of resources in favour of the more immediately threatening Western and Eastern Fronts, the troops in Italy fought intelligently and stubbornly, making the Allies pay the highest cost in blood and material before falling back to the next prepared defensive line.

In this theatre the troops were equipped with a mixture of the classic field grey temperate uniform, tropical uniform, camouflage items, and confiscated Italian stocks.

1—Field grey mountain cap, modelled originally on that of the Austrian *'Gebirgsjäger'* of the Great War. The German *Gebirgsjäger* started the war as the only troops wearing this classic headgear; but it was copied in 1941 for the new tropical field cap of the *Afrika Korps,* and in 1943 a very similar pattern became the standard everyday headgear of the *Wehrmacht*, replacing the sidecap. The mountain cap has a slightly higher outline and shorter peak than the later types. There are two ventilation eyelets; and the band, which can be folded down to protect the face, fastens with two front buttons. The national eagle-and-swastika in grey on green, and the national cockade, are displayed on the front of the crown; and the metal branch-of-service badge, an edelweiss flower, is pinned to the left side.

2—Tropical shirt in olive cotton.

3—Tropical tunic, of the simplified type which appeared in 1942/43, of looser cut and with unpleated pockets. The original olive shade became very faded in use; there was also occasional use of *Luftwaffe* equivalents, which were made in pale sand-khaki. The usual removable shoulder straps of tropical pattern bear the mid-green piping of the mountain troops. The illustrated example of the branch's edelweiss sleeve patch is in tropical pattern, embroidered in white on brown; the Army's breast eagle is in tropical blue and brown. Insignia from the woollen uniform, in standard colours, were often seen attached to tropical clothing in Italy.

4—Equipment suspenders in webbing, produced for tropical use but often seen on the mainland of Europe in 1943/45. The original colour was light olive, but the webbing faded with use to tan yellow.

5—Cartridge pouches in canvas and leather, each of the pair holding two magazines for the semi-automatic *Gewehr 43* rifle; the colours and exact materials varied. These pouches were in short supply, and often a rifleman had to use one pair of canvas pouches for the detachable magazines, and one set of three standard pouches holding loose rounds or clips of cartridges.

6—M1942 steel helmet, camouflage-painted to match the terrain on this front.

7—Standard issue belt.

8—M1931 'breadbag'.

9—Water bottle, here a large one-litre version theoretically reserved for stretcher-bearers, but a popular item in Italy among any troops who could lay hands on them.

10—Straight-cut cotton trousers. They have two side pockets, one with a buttoned flap on the right rear, and an integral belt with a three-prong buckle.

11—Short puttees, specific to the mountain troops on all fronts; a small hook held them down on the boots.

12—Mountain boots, heavily nailed, made of natural leather with a top strip of field grey cloth.

13—*Gewehr 43* semi-automatic rifle, in 7.92mm calibre, with a detachable ten-round magazine; this was an efficient weapon, but it was never available in large numbers, and its hurrying into service led to frequent malfunctions.

14—ZF4 telescopic sight, x4.

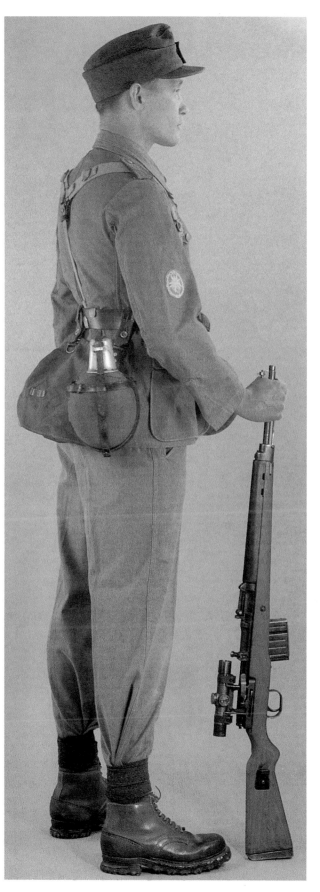

US ARMY AUTOMATIC RIFLEMAN, ENGLAND AND NORMANDY, JUNE 1944

Depicted as he embarks for the Normandy landings of June 1944, this squad automatic rifleman represents the typical GI of the last year of the war in Europe. There had been a certain amount of modification of individual items, and the introduction of some new materials; but the basic outfit had not changed significantly since the entry of the USA into the war.

1—M1 steel helmet, which had officially replaced the M1917 (of British shape) in June 1941. Apart from its very modern shape, still in use today all round the world, the M1 had another unique feature: its construction in two parts. The outer steel shell, to which the main chinstrap was fixed, fitted exactly over a slightly smaller shell of the same shape but made of a laminated fibre material. The internal harness of fabric straps which gripped the head was fixed inside the light 'liner', which was often worn without the shell when out of battle. Here the two-part webbing chinstrap of the shell (rarely fastened in battle) is tucked into the camouflage net.

2—M1941 knitted woollen cap, or 'beanie'. This could be worn under the helmet in cold weather, or worn alone as a casual off-duty headgear. It has a short stiffened front brim, and the sides and rear can be folded down over the ears.

3—Wool shirt, worn here over a white T-shirt; it had two patch breast pockets, and could be worn with a necktie for walking-out. An internal flap could be buttoned across inside the neck, supposedly as added protection against gas.

4—M1941 field jacket, made of beige cotton/poplin lined with olive flannel. This windcheater-style jacket, consciously modelled on civilian sportswear, was an important innovation: the first major example of the universal issue in one of the world's great armies of a garment specifically for field wear, replacing the all-purpose woollen service-and-combat tunics worn by other armies. It fastens with a front zip covered by a buttoned fly; buttoned tabs secure the collar and wrists, and others gather the waist; two large vertical pleats behind the shoulders give easy fitting. The M1941 did betray shortcomings in service, however. It was comfortable in temperate weather, but was too light for northern winters, and too hot in summer; and its two slash pockets had no useful carrying capacity. The example illustrated bears on the left shoulder the divisional patch of the famous 2nd Infantry Division 'Indianhead', which landed on Omaha Beach on D+1 and D+2, and fought across Europe to finish the war at Leipzig.

5—The old M1928 'haversack' had inadequate capacity, and it was eventually replaced by the M1944 and M1945 combat and cargo packs, each being a two-part pack with a small knapsack for combat use and a detachable lower bag for full marching order. In fact, few of these new packs arrived in the line before VE-Day, and most troops soldiered on with the M1928, purpose bag below it for the tent equipment and changes of clothes. Our subject still has the uncomfortable World War I 'pack carrier' attached below the haversack, holding his sleeping gear: he will certainly ditch it at the first opportunity after landing. The haversack held rations, washing kit, etc.; the pocket on its flap held the mess kit, and the M1910 entrenching pick is attached under it here. It is a sign of the inadequacy of the pack system that this soldier has tied his blanket to it with cord; the M1944 system had proper stowage straps. He also has the US Navy M1926 'life belt' issued to troops for the Channel crossing to Normandy (which proved completely useless); and – copied from a famous photograph – the regulation model bugle, a romantically anachronistic touch in 1944.

6—M4 gasmask in its M6 satchel – regulation equipment at all times, but cumbersome, the gasmask was often thrown away and its bag retained as a general purpose haversack.

7—M1937 automatic rifleman's belt, with six pouches each holding two of the detachable 20-round magazines for the Browning Automatic Rifle – the US equivalent of the Bren. The belt's eyelets were compatible with the rest of the web equipment; hooked to it here are the M1942 field dressing pouch at right front, the M1938 wirecutters on the left, and the M1910 water bottle carrier at the rear.

8—Browning Automatic Rifle M1918A2, calibre .30-06, with M1907 standard leather rifle sling.

9—Wool trousers, in 'olive drab', as introduced in 1937. For much of the war the GI wore these all-purpose uniform trousers with the field jacket.

10—M1938 web leggings, laced up the outside and with a strap passing under the boot.

11—Standard issue natural leather ankle boots with rubber heels and soles; the leather was used 'rough side out'.

GERMAN INFANTRYMAN, NORMANDY, SUMMER 1944

In the summer of 1944, fighting on three fronts under skies ruled by the Allies, the *Wehrmacht* was beginning to suffer from serious shortages. The *'Landser'* of this last year of the war, though his fighting quality remained high, presented a picture of forced economy and compromise. His uniform, of simplified cut, was made of a mixed material with a high content of 'shoddy'; it was less robust than before, and its colour tended more towards a brownish grey than the classic field grey. Leather equipment was increasingly replaced by various *'ersatz'* equivalents made of cheaper fabrics. By contrast, his weapons were becoming ever more efficient, and he faced the swarming Allied armour with the best infantry anti-tank weapon of the whole war: the one-shot *'Panzerfaust'*.

1—M1943 field cap, bearing the Army's eagle-and-swastika and cockade on a grey patch on the front of the crown. This cap, modelled on the mountain cap but of lower outline and with a longer peak, began to replace the sidecap in 1943; although the sidecap was still to be seen in individual cases up until the end of the war, by mid-1944 the peaked version was very widely worn by all ranks up to and including generals.

2—M1943 shirt, in grey-green material, with three front buttons and two buttoned breast pockets. When in shirtsleeve order the removable tunic shoulder straps could be worn on the shirt.

3—Field grey tunic, of 1943/44 manufacture. Simplified for economy, it has unpleated pockets with simpler-shaped flaps, and a field grey collar in place of the earlier green. The shade tended away from green-grey toward ash-grey or a brownish-grey. The standard collar 'lace' is now in mouse-grey, without branch-of-service distinction; the Army breast eagle above the right pocket is also grey on grey, rather than white on green. The ribbon in his second buttonhole is that of the Iron Cross 2nd Class. The shoulder straps, in field grey now instead of green, bear white infantry branch piping.

4—Equipment suspenders M1939.

5—M1933 rifle cartridge pouches.

6—M1924 hand grenade.

7—M1939 'egg' grenade.

8—M1935 helmet, in a cover looped for foliage and held tight by a lace or an elastic; it is made of the same 'splinter' camouflage material as the M1931 tent section/poncho.

9—M1939 assault pack frame, here stowed with the mess tin, above the M1931 *Zeltbahn*, which hides the lower bag containing iron rations, sweater, tent pegs, etc.

10—M1938 gasmask and gascape.

11—M1931 water bottle.

12—Entrenching tool.

13—M1931 'breadbag'.

14—M1943 straight-cut trousers, with straps under the feet.

15—Rare at this date, the shortened marching boots dating from late 1939; by this date the ankle boots and canvas gaiters were more common.

16—Mauser 98k rifle, 7.92mm calibre. This standard weapon remained in use right through the war.

17—*'Panzerfaust 60'* single-shot 'throw-away' anti-tank rocket launcher. Its 6lb. explosive head could penetrate any tank of the period at short range; and in the Normandy hedgerows and the ruins of European towns, most fighting was at short range. The tube was rested across the shoulder, and the warhead was aimed with simple flip-up sights (painted phosphorescent for night use).

BRITISH INFANTRYMAN, NORMANDY, JUNE 1944

This soldier of the 3rd 'Iron' Division, one of the first ashore on Sword Beach on 6 June 1944, wears a uniform basically unchanged since 1940, but with certain items of equipment dating from the invasion preparations of 1943.

1—Mk.III steel helmet, of the 'tortoise' shape worn by the Tommy until the 1980s. This was developed in 1942, but first seen in any numbers in Normandy; it was issued while stocks of Mk.II helmets were still plentiful, and both were worn side by side within infantry units until the end of the war.

2—Rubberised canvas groundsheet/rain cape, rolled and tied at the top of the assault jerkin.

3—Blouse of the 1940 pattern Battledress in khaki serge, varying from the pre-war model in having unpleated pockets and visible plastic buttons. This man, like many in Normandy, wears a full set of sleeve insignia; officially this was to be removed for security reasons, but photographs show that practice varied widely from unit to unit. At the top of the sleeve is the regimental title, in white on scarlet for Guards and line infantry – here, that of the South Lancashire Regiment, whose 1st Battalion served in 3rd Division. Below the title is the black and red divisional sign, its triangular sections a reference to '3'. Infantry units wore red felt strips, their number indicating the senior, second, and junior brigades within the division – here, the senior brigade. Below this he wears corporal's chevrons. All insignia appeared on both sleeves.

4—Rubberised inflatable 'life belt' issued for the landing operation. It was largely of psychological value, since it would not save a heavily burdened man.

5—The 1943 'light respirator' in its satchel; unlike the old box type, this had a filter screwed on to the side of the face mask. The satchel also contained cheap cellophane anti-gas goggles, ointment, anti-misting wipes for the eye pieces, etc.

6—The short-lived 1942 'battle jerkin' developed by Col. Rivers-Macpherson, and issued only to some of the initial assault waves for D-Day. It was supposed to give more flexible stowage of necessary equipment, better weight distribution, and the advantage of being put on or discarded in one piece. Of waterproof brown cotton duck material, it could accommodate a great deal of kit. Ammunition and magazines for all standard small arms, grenades, mortar bombs, etc. could be carried in the front pockets; grenades and 2in. mortar bombs could also be carried in the side pockets; there were attachments for the bayonet and a fighting knife; the two large rear pockets held iron rations, mess kit, gascape, entrenching tool, and more ammunition; 'sleeves', straps and cords could be used to attach a machete, pistol holster, and other extra items, and there were inside pockets for maps and other soft kit. This soldier has attached his enamelled mug to the rear, and has a 'toggle rope' – typical of the assault troops – round his neck and shoulders.

7—Lee Enfield Rifle No. 4 Mk.I; a development of the classic .303in. SMLE, it was a pre-war design but was not issued in numbers until 1942. It was improved over the SMLE in various matters of detail, but had essentially the same performance. The small 'spike' bayonet fitted over the protruding muzzle, which was the immediate distinguishing feature. The standard weapon for a corporal section leader was the Sten submachine gun; but it is entirely likely that an experienced NCO going into battle would prefer the accurate, reliable, if heavy rifle over the flimsy, dangerously unreliable, and very short-range Sten.

8—Pattern 1940 Battledress trousers; the economy model had exposed pocket buttons, and no belt loops or ankle tabs.

9—'Anklets, web' entirely in cotton webbing, including the straps.

10—Hobnailed 'ammunition boots'.

Philippe Charbonnier

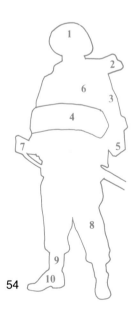

WAFFEN-SS INFANTRY NCO, NORMANDY, SUMMER 1944

The Allied troops who fought their way ashore on D-Day faced variable resistance, some of the German units in the coastal defence zone being of less than impressive quality. But the liberators were faced, within hours, by some of the most formidable divisions in the *Wehrmacht*: first-class *Waffen-SS* armour and infantry, rushed to the new front as Hitler's 'fire brigade'. Bitterly resisting the Allied advance through the massive hedgerows and small banked fields of Normandy, and throwing in savage counterattacks as long as they could scrape together even a weak company and a handful of tanks, the *Waffen-SS* made the Allies pay dearly for every yard of French soil. Their appearance represented an *ad hoc* mixture of the classic uniform items with camouflage garments, and *ersatz* personal equipment.

1—Field grey sidecap, adopted in 1940, with the special *Waffen-SS* shape of eagle-and-swastika insignia, and the SS death's-head replacing the Army's national cockade, the badges embroidered in silver-grey on black. This cap style had been replaced a year before by the peaked type; but was still seen quite widely, particularly among veteran soldiers.

2—Shirt with collar, and two buttoned, flapped breast pockets, introduced in place of the old collarless type in 1943. It could be worn with a tie, and with tunic shoulder straps when in shirtsleeve order.

3—Late war model of the tunic, officially field grey, although the high shoddy content in the cloth made for colour distortions. Note simplified pockets, and field grey collar, characteristic of tunics from 1943. The right hand collar patch bears the runes of the SS; the left one bears a silver metal pip, identifying the rank of '*Unterscharführer*' (senior corporal or junior sergeant); and the front and bottom edges of the collar itself bear the silver-grey braid of NCOs from this rank upward. On the left upper arm is the SS-shape eagle-and-swastika badge; on the forearm, the cuff title of the 17th SS Panzer-Grenadier Division '*Götz von Berlichingen*', which fought around Carentan and Avranches in Normandy. On the upper right arm is an award badge indicating the single-handed destruction of an enemy tank with an infantry weapon, e.g. a *Panzerfaust*. On the right pocket is the embroidered star of the German Cross in Gold award, unusual for an NCO. A whistle lanyard emerges from his pocket.

4—Standard M1939 leather equipment suspenders.

5—Binoculars, 6x30, painted in the dull ochre used for German vehicles and many items of equipment from 1943/44.

6—M1924 hand grenade.

7—Pair of triple magazine pouches for the MP40 sub-machine gun, in canvas with leather fittings, with attachments for the belt and suspenders. The left hand set has a small external pocket for tools.

8—Standard belt with SS-specific buckle plate bearing the SS eagle and the motto '*Meine Ehre heisst Treue*' — 'My Honour is Loyalty'.

9—Rubber lens protector for the binoculars.

10—*Zeltbahn* shelter half in SS camouflage pattern.

11—Binocular case in dark brown bakelite.

12—M1931 'breadbag'.

13—M1931 water bottle.

14—M1935 helmet, with SS camouflage cover.

15—Straight trousers in camouflage material, of the so-called 'pea' pattern, adopted by the *Waffen-SS* only; these were the trousers of the complete 1944 camouflage uniform, issued with a jacket cut in the same shape as the woollen tunic. The uniform could be worn over the wool uniform, or instead of it in hot weather. Mixed uniforms, as here, were not uncommon in the field.

16—Standard issue socks, here rolled for lack of gaiters.

17—Standard ankle boots of natural leather; they were often seen blackened.

18—The MP40 sub-machine gun in 9mm calibre, the famous '*Schmeisser*'; note folding skeleton butt. This was one of the finest SMGs to appear during the war, and was eagerly sought after by soldiers of both sides.

PRIVATE, US 2ND RANGER BATTALION, NORMANDY, JUNE 1944

Our subject represents one of the picked Ranger infantrymen who made the daring assault on the cliff-top battery at Pointe du Hoc, commanding both Utah and Omaha Beaches, on the morning of 6 June. Companies D, E and F of the battalion, commanded by Lt.Col. Rudder, climbed sheer cliffs under heavy fire; captured the battery (from which the 155mm guns were found to have been removed); and held the position for two days against heavy counterattacks. He wears various equipment specific to the Normandy landings and not carried thereafter.

1—M1943 tinted goggles, for protection against sun, dust and spray.

2—M1 steel helmet, with the 2nd Ranger Battalion's insignia painted on the back, for identification by following troops.

3—M5 amphibious assault gasmask. This was a light, short-term use item in a waterproof carrier, to be fixed wherever convenient on the equipment.

4—M1941 field jacket over wool shirt. The insignia common to the Ranger battalions is sewn to the left shoulder.

5—Assault vest. The US equivalent of the British 'battle jerkin', very similar in its layout, capacity, and construction, but in the normal US equipment materials and with attachments for fastening standard US webbing items, e.g. the carrier for the M1943 entrenching tool. An M18 smoke grenade is carried on the left hip, and rope on the back.

6—Gas-detecting brassard, in a treated material which changed colour in the presence of gas.

7—M1936 pistol belt, to which are attached: M1923 double magazine pouch for the automatic pistol (front), double magazine pouch for the M1 carbine, M1910 water bottle, M1942 field dressing pouch, M3 knife, and M1911A1 Colt .45 cal. automatic pistol in M1916 holster.

8—M1 carbine, with 20-round magazine. Despite its drawbacks, this weapon was favoured by light assault troops (e.g. paratroopers) over the heavier M1 Garand rifle.

9—The herringbone twill utility fatigues were sometimes used as combat clothing in Europe, often over the wool uniform in cold weather. The trousers are worn here; their large cargo pockets, on the outside of the thighs, were useful in the field. The M1943 combat fatigues were not yet widely available in NW Europe; and, oddly, the trousers of that suit lacked the useful cargo pockets.

10—M1938 web leggings.

11—Standard ankle boots in natural leather, matt side out, with rubber heels and soles.

Philippe Charbonnier

WAFFEN-SS INFANTRYMAN, ARDENNES, DECEMBER 1944

After the Allied breakout from Normandy and the subsequent rapid advance across France, the liberators were checked in Holland and Belgium partly by a revived German resistance, and partly by the fact that they had outrun their armies' ability to supply their massive logistic needs. On 16 December 1944 the German forces launched a last major counter-offensive in the Ardennes; their last reserves in the West of tanks, SS units, paratroopers, and other less formidable troops were thrown into a drive through the snow-covered hills with the aim of reaching the Channel and cutting the Allies in two. A mixture of survivors from Normandy and new replacements, the assaulting divisions presented a motley appearance, and by no means all of them were properly equipped for winter warfare; they looted American depots whenever opportunity offered.

1—M1943 field cap, the *Waffen-SS* insignia here separated in characteristic fashion – there was no room for both eagle and death's-head on the front of the crown above the flap. Some SS troops received a smaller version of the insignia woven together on a triangular grey patch, worn on the front of the cap.

2—Standard issue 'toque', a simple woollen tube worn in various ways over the head and neck in cold weather.

3—Jacket of the 1944 *Waffen-SS* camouflage uniform, which aped the cut of the woollen service dress. It has four simple pockets and an open collar, and could be worn alone or, as here, over the woollen uniform. The *Waffen-SS* version of the national emblem was very often worn on the left sleeve; the uniform shoulder straps were often added as well; and there was a simplified system of sleeve rank insignia involving green bars on black horizontal patches which were sometimes seen on this uniform as an alternative to the rank shoulder straps. This 1944 camouflage uniform, unlike all previous equivalents, was non-reversible.

4—Standard M1939 equipment suspenders.

5—Wooden-hilted combat knife, with a spring hook on the sheath allowing it to be worn either on a belt or strap, in the boot top, or in the front of the tunic.

6—Pair of triple magazine pouches for the StG44 assault rifle. They were made in canvas of various shades, often with leather reinforcement. The heavy weight of the six large box magazines – 14lbs. when fully loaded – required an adjustable strap linking the pouches behind the back, to prevent them falling forward.

7—Standard belt with SS buckle.

8—M1924 hand grenade.

9—Camouflaged *Zeltbahn* shelter half, here strapped directly to the D-rings of the equipment suspenders.

10—M1931 breadbag.

11—M1931 water bottle, attached to the breadbag.

12—M1931 mess tin, attached to the breadbag.

13—Entrenching tool carrier in artificial leather.

14—Mauser M1884/98 bayonet.

15—Trousers of the 1944 SS camouflage uniform, cut like the 1942 woollen trousers.

16—Standard issue grey wool knitted gloves.

17—Short webbing gaiters.

18—Standard ankle boots.

19—*Sturmgewehr* M1944, in calibre '7.92mm short'. A revolutionary weapon, this was the ancestor of all today's 'assault rifles' – i.e. weapons of small calibre firing a short, powerful round, with a fully automatic capability, to replace both the rifle and the sub-machine gun in the soldier's armoury. Mass produced from cheap stampings, it was rather vulnerable to hard field use; and the reliable provision of the new ammunition was difficult for a beleaguered army disorganised by defeat on two fronts.

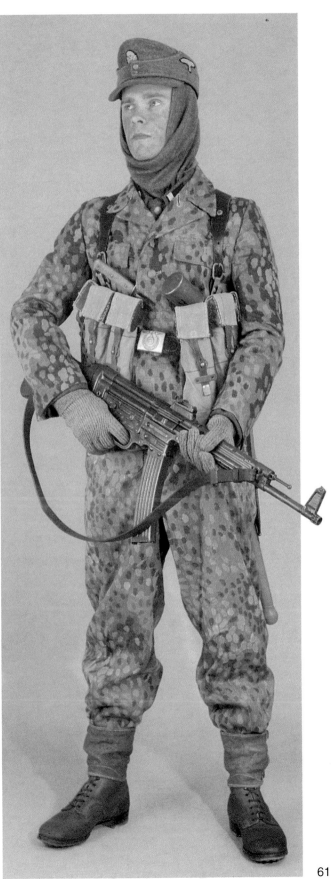

STAFF SERGEANT, US ARMY INFANTRY, GERMANY, SPRING 1945

This platoon NCO, wearing light equipment for a patrol or assault after leaving his pack in the unit transport, represents both the final appearance of the GI in Europe, and the type of combat uniform which would spread across the world in the post-war years. The M1943 combat/fatigue uniform, in greenish olive cotton poplin, was windproof and (to a limited extent) waterproof. It was of practical design, the jacket having plenty of large pockets; and, by varying the layers of clothing worn beneath it, it could be worn comfortably in all seasons.

1—M1 steel helmet, worn over the knitted 'beanie' cap, and covered with the recently issued small-mesh camouflage net held by an elasticated band. The chin-straps were often left loose, or tucked up, in action: the blast of a nearby explosion could catch the helmet and snap the neck if the straps were fastened.

2—The buttoned collar of the very popular olive wool knitted sweater. The layering principle rested on the wear of the outer fatigue garments to give protection only against wind and rain, over various inner garments for warmth: a vest, flannel shirt, and sweater. This system, which replaced the vain attempts to design a uniform equally suitable for field and service wear, was later copied the world over.

3—The M1943 combat/fatigue jacket. It has four large pockets; buttoned tabs at the wrist and collar; a buttoned front covered by a fly; an internal waist tightening cord; and an optional button-on hood. A separate winter lining – in short supply – could be buttoned into place inside the jacket. The divisional patch (here the yellow 'Thunderbird' on a red diamond of the 45th Infantry Division) and NCO chevrons and 'rockers' are sewn to the left shoulder and both upper arms respectively.

4—M1936 pistol belt and web shoulder suspenders; the belt carries the M1910 canteen in its fabric carrier (note the green tint of US webbing issued new from 1943); a five-magazine pouch rig for the box magazines now issued with the Thompson sub-machine gun; the M1943 entrenching tool; and a compass pouch. An electric torch (TL122C) with angled head, and a Mk.II defensive hand grenade, are attached to the M1936 suspenders.

5—Wool gloves with leather palm and finger reinforcement.

6—The M6 satchel for the M4 gasmask, which has probably been discarded long ago, leaving the satchel to act as a useful field 'carry-all' haversack.

7—Thompson M1A1 .45 calibre sub-machine gun, a simplified version of the M1928A1 most immediately recognisable by the substitution of a plain wooden forearm for the front pistol grip, and the absence of the muzzle compensator. It was now issued with 20- and 30-round box magazines. This was still the junior leader's regulation weapon, despite the appearance of the lighter M3 'grease gun', and its massive stopping-power was still appreciated in close-quarter battle.

8—Trousers of the M1943 combat/fatigue suit, usually issued one size too large so that they could be worn over the wool trousers. They could be worn with either belt or suspenders, and a buttoning tab gathered the ankle.

9—M1943 'double buckle' combat boots, which began to replace earlier ankle boots and web leggings in 1944. They still did not give much protection against cold or wet; but the integral leather gaiter-flaps, fastened with two buckled straps, were much more convenient than the long laced leggings.

Philippe Charbonnier

63

GERMAN INFANTRYMAN, BERLIN, APRIL-MAY 1945

As the shadows closed over the 3rd Reich, the German infantryman presented a very different appearance from his counterpart in the victorious early campaigns. Only the classic helmet remained unchanged. Despite all difficulties, German industry continued to supply the *Wehrmacht* with necessary equipment, although economy forced radical redesign of some items, and much *ersatz* material.

The final uniform adopted by the Army and *Waffen-SS* was modelled on the Battledress of the advancing Tommies. Since this was a notoriously uncomfortable uniform to wear in battle (the blouse and trousers always parted company when the soldier exerted himself in any way), economy was the only motive. Various shades of grey cloth were used in its manufacture, including not only German 'shoddy' but also captured Russian and Italian stocks, and the result was fairly motley. Only the German soldier's weapons remained of first class quality; and in the ruins of Berlin the StG44 and the *Panzerfaust* took a high final toll of the invading Red Army.

1—M1942 helmet, painted matt grey, without a cover; note that the decal insignia had long since been abandoned.

2—M1943 shirt with turn-down collar and two breast pockets.

3—M1944 blouse, this example made from a kind of gabardine, probably of Italian or Czechoslovak origin. It has two unpleated patch pockets with straight flaps. The shirt collar hides, in this instance, the 'lace' on the collar, which was still of the plain grey design used since 1943. The short-cut blouse has a broad waist band with two buttons. The standard shoulder straps are still attached, here with the white piping of the infantry; and the national eagle is still worn on the right breast, in grey on a green-grey triangular patch. The ribbon of the Iron Cross 2nd Class is worn in the buttonhole.

4—M1939 equipment suspender. Examples in fabric were also issued towards the end of the war.

5—Standard issue belt and buckle plate.

6—Pair of triple magazine pouches for the StG44 rifle. These appeared in various materials, although the basic design was the same. Khaki-yellow canvas pouches were the most common, although pale blue-grey or olive canvas was also used, and rubberised fabric sometimes replaced the artificial leather fittings seen here.

7—M1931 camouflaged shelter half or *Zeltbahn*, unchanged throughout the war.

8—M1938 gasmask in its fluted container. This item, which was completely useless owing to the fact that gas was never used in battle throughout the war, was nevertheless regulation issue until the end of hostilities. The mask itself was often discarded, and the canister used for carrying other items.

9—The anti-gas cape was equally useless in its intended function; its only practical use was as a field shroud for front-line dead.

10—Late example of the M1931 breadbag, of simplified construction.

11—M1931 water bottle.

12—Entrenching spade in its yellowish artificial leather carrier, typical of the last period of the war.

13—M1944 straight-cut trousers, of the same Italian or Czech fabric as the blouse illustrated. Of loose cut, with an integral belt, they had two rear pockets, two slash side pockets, and a front fob pocket. Since the M1944 blouse had no internal pocket in the lining for the field dressing carried inside the skirt of the old full-length tunic, this item was now fixed inside the right side of the trousers. The trouser legs were gathered at the ankle by a lace.

14—Short canvas gaiters.

15—Ankle boots.

16—StG44 assault rifle.

This edition published
in Great Britain 1999 by
The Crowood Press Ltd.
Ramsbury, Marlborough
Wiltshire SN8 2HR

Printed in Singapore

British Library Cataloguing in Publication Data
Mirouze, Laurent
World War II infantry in colour photographs – (Europa-
militaria; 2)
1. Armies. Infantry. History
1. Title II. Series
326'.1'09

ISBN 1 86126 287 6

Acknowledgements:
The assembly of such a large number of original World War II
uniforms and equipment items would have been impossible
without the generous help of many collections, private and
public. We wish to express our gratitude for their co-operation
to:
British & US Armies Jacques Alluchon, Pierre Besnard ('Le
Poilu'), Jean Bouchery, Eric Bouteloup, Hubert de Belleville,
Philippe Charbonnier, Christophe Deschodt, Raphael
Destombes, Luc Fauconnier, Frédéric Finel ('Overlord'), Hervé
Halfen, Régis Le Cap, Christian Lefèvre, Eric Martin, Jean-Yves
Nasse, Olivier Reinbold, Jean Rocheteau, Hugues Rougé.
German Army Eric Lefèvre, Jean de Lagarde. *French Army*
Eric Hernandez, François Vauvillier. *Italian Army* Furio
Lazzarini, Franco Mesturini. *Soviet & Japanese Armies* Gérard
Gorokhoff. *Polish Army* Jan Rutkiewicz, and Messrs. Hieronim
and Przemyslaw Kroczynski of the Polish Army Museum,
Colberg. *Belgian Army* Musée Royal de l'Armée, Brussels, and
its curator M. Jacobs.

Photo credits
Lech Alexandrovicz (p.5); Tony Bergamo (pp. 15, 21, 25, 47);
Philippe Charbonnier (p.41); Stefan Ciejka (pp. 7, 17, 23, 27,
29, 31, 33, 35, 39, 53, 57, 61, 65); Laurent Mirouze (pp.11, 13,
19, 37, 45, 51, 55, 59, 63); François Vauvillier (pp.9,43).